On *Vermont* Time ...

Musings, Essays, Short Stories, Poems,
Drawings and Photos

All depicting a little bit about life
in the Green Mountains of Vermont

An Anthology Compiled and Edited By:
Timothy G. Stetson

**Featuring the writings,
poems, drawings and photos of:**

Timothy G. Stetson ... Lou Hill ... Roderick Bates ...
Lauren Young ... Kraig McFadden ... Harold Green ...
and Gardner Stetson

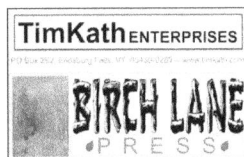

TimKath ENTERPRISES

BIRCH LANE
PRESS

ISBN: 978-0-9727115-1-7

Birch Lane Press
Division of TimKath Enterprises
PO Box 282
Enosburg Falls, VT 05450
(802) 933-2513

Acknowledgements

In the process of writing and compiling this book there are tons of people that I must acknowledge and I hope not to forget anyone, so for all of you that over the years have provided me with ideas and information and have been the impetus for my writing … Thank You, Thank You, Thank You.

I especially want to thank my friend Lou Hill's wife Gwen and his daughter Lesli Blount who graciously agreed to allow me to publish Lou's works in this book and have worked tirelessly all through the project to help me bring the book to the state of publication. Gwen and Lesli provided me with a ton of the extra inspiration necessary to undertake a project like this one

I really want to thank my wife Kathy who supports me wholeheartedly on the many projects that I undertake. Honey… I actually have finished one complete book.

I also want to thank all those other authors, poets, and artists who agreed to be included in the book. This project is not one of those projects that any one of us sets out to make "huge money" on. It is a project of love for the state we live in and the history of that state and our life in it.

Most of all I would like to thank you for purchasing this book and adding it to your library. I sure hope that you find it to be a fun read and that you learn a little about a part of the country that I, my family and friends just love living in … the Green Mountains of Vermont. I also hope that you enjoy meeting my friend Lou Hill whom all of us miss each and every day. He always had a story and I am so pleased to be able to share them with all of you. In addition I am so happy to have been joined by Roderick Bates, Lauren Young, and Kraig McFadden on this project and being able to include photos from my father Gardner Stetson and father-in-law Harold Green.

Enjoy the journey … "On Vermont Time…"

Table of Contents

Introduction

Welcome to "On Vermont Time…" a compendium, an anthology, all right a collection of musings, essays, short stories, poems and photos all about Vermont or at least connected to the Vermont way of life in one form or another.

It is a book that has really been written over an extended period of time by many different people from many different perspectives. At various points in the project I really wondered if I would ever complete the project but here it is.

As I sit here and write this introduction it is the day after Christmas 2011 (which gives you an idea of how long it took as we published in 2013) and this Christmas I received a gift bag from my sister and brother-in-law that I think put in perspective the answer to the question many ask … Why a book called "On Vermont Time?" My gift bag included some Maple Apple Wine from the Boyden Farms Winery in Cambridge, some pickles canned by a local vendor and a book called "Off The Beaten Path® Vermont…*A Guide to Unique Places*". As I opened the gift bag, my brother-in-law let me know that after going traveling with my wife Kathy and I this past summer, while we were camping, that it was an easy decision to purchase the items in it. I took them to many of the "hidden" gems that are the Green Mountains of Vermont. I hope, if nothing else, that this book will entice you to come and visit us here in Vermont if you don't already live here and if you do live here to sit back and remember why we all choose to stay here in this wonderful, beautiful state.

So sit back, kick up your feet and enjoy the trip to the past, the present and the future in the Green Mountains … "On Vermont Time…"

1

On Vermont Time ...

Chapter 1

Autumn in Enosburg Falls, Vermont
"On Vermont Time..."

By Timothy G. Stetson

This is the first in a series of stories that I originally published on the internet about the little Green Mountain Village of Enosburg Falls, Vermont tucked in the northern portion of the state, just 7 miles from the Canadian Border. I hope you find the time to come and visit our little village and spend a little while "On Vermont Time." If you can't come to us...I hope these stories bring us a little closer to you and provide you with some relaxing enjoyment.

The crickets are chirping, the air is cool, but it is still warm enough to be comfortable without a jacket. I can hear the water in the garden pond splashing over the rocks, playing the ever-famous soothing tune of running water. Great for stress relief, I'm told. It's a cool fall morning in Northern Vermont.

The moths and other insects fly around the outside light, on the garage, as soon as it comes on and glistens in the morning dew. They are enjoying the time they have left before the cold of winter sets in.

The stars in the sky don't show this morning and you can't quite see Jay Peak. The weather forecasters are telling us to expect rain today and maybe through the rest of the week. Still, it's a typical fall day in Vermont.

Some of the leaves are just starting to change. Soon, the woods and mountains will be covered with a canvas of color.

Old-time Vermonters still say it's early for the leaves to change, but we know that Mother Nature will have them change when the time is right.

Soon, we hope, the buses filled with visitors from communities all over the country and maybe even the world will start to make their way into the state weaving around and over its mountainous terrain and taking in the autumn show of the changing trees. "Leaf Peepers" as they are affectionately called, are a welcome site in Vermont, especially to the little villages like the one I live in, Enosburg Falls, where tourism is still important to our economy.

We hope you come and visit and enjoy our little community. There's a lot to do here during the year and especially in the fall. We still have farms of all different sizes that you can see and even some that you can stop and visit on your way through.

The Farmers Market still goes on every Saturday morning on Lincoln Park, right in the center of the village. You can purchase all of the harvest goodies from a summer of planting, weeding and harvesting. While you are on the park, you can check out our town bandstand where the Enosburg Falls Town Band plays every Tuesday night during the summer months. It is also used by other groups throughout the summer from the Vermont Dairy Festival in spring to the American Legion at those times during the year when we celebrate our veterans. As you look across the park, you will also see a little log cabin sitting right across the road from the bandstand. If you come back in the summer and visit us, you can take in the band concert on a Tuesday night and go over and visit the log cabin. There is a lot of Enosburg and Vermont History right here in this building.

All of our main street merchants are also open. You can visit the antique stores, children's and men's clothing stores, drug & variety stores, restaurants, cafes, and if you still need that miscellaneous nut, screw, or bolt for some repair to your vehicle or something you brought with you, check in at one of our four hardware stores.

If you are interested in history, especially New England or Vermont history, Enosburg has lots of it to share. You can start out at our 1892 Opera House. It was built, for our community, by the B.J. Kendall Company as a community hall. The B.J. Kendall Co. owned the Spavin Cure that Enosburg is famous for. The Spavin Cure building, itself, is still standing at the north end of the village. Since the Opera House was built, there have been all kinds of performances and community events held here. There is a major renovation project currently underway which is making one of our favorite buildings even better. I will be doing an article on the Opera House itself sometime real soon, so be sure to check back for that.

You can also visit our historical society museums. Museum(s), you say? Yes, currently the Enosburg Historical Society has 2; One on Main Street, upstairs over our Town Hall and one right across the road from the Opera House. This one is in an old train freight station and has a real caboose parked right next to it. The "new" museum is still being finished up but has all kinds of great history to share with you.

What else is there to do, you ask? We have a bridge of flowers and lights; built over the dam on the Missisquoi River that generates electricity from the awesome power of water. We have The Somerset Inn, which at one time was called the Quincy Hotel, where you can go and eat and enjoy the quiet and quaintness of the Green Mountains in autumn. Just to see the old houses that are still here after all these years is a trip unto itself.

This is only the beginning, just a taste to whet your appetite for more. We have Bed & Breakfasts, beautiful Churches and many other sites to behold. Be sure to check out my stories over the next few months as I share more information about our little village, the county, the State of Vermont and the people that live here.

We do hope that you will find time to come and visit us and spend a little while "On Vermont Time..."

Summer Ensemble

Poetry by Lauren L. Young

Purple Vetch & Orange Paintbrushes
Whispers of a Breeze
Swaying Grass
Daisies & Buttercups

Mountains Look
Blue Sky
Faces in the Clouds
Sun, Yellow, Warm

Nature Resounds
Instruments Tune
Symphony Explodes
Encore! Encore!

Fluting Tongues
Playing Fingers
Escalating Joy
Sheer Ecstasy

Beauty to Behold
Deafening Rhythm
Soaring
Orchestra Finale

Gleaming Rays of Gold
Shimmering Light
Wings of Love
Meadow Masterpiece

Chapter 2

A Day in November
"On Vermont Time…"

By Timothy G. Stetson

It's a beautiful November Sunday morning in Vermont. The sky is blue with only a few stragglers in the "cloud-scape." The air is crisp and there is a dusting of about 3" of snow blanketing the ground. The fragrance of wood smoke fills the air as the heaviness of the morning atmosphere lifts to let in the sun.

At our house, the smell of Green Mountain Coffee Roasters coffee fills the air and down in the family room our oldest son is lighting our new Pellet Stove. "A pellet stove you ask?" Yes, a pellet stove. Who in the world would have thought that the day would come when we would be burning pelletized sawdust but it's here. With the economy being in kind of a tough place many people are switching to burning wood products once again. I know that isn't new for northern New England but quite a few people that didn't burn wood before are now turning to it in an effort to save money. For many the good choice has been wood pellets.

For our family, we always wished that we had put in a chimney and a wood stove when we built the house but for a lot of reasons then we didn't. Because the pellet stove is a direct-vent type of wood burning stove they can be put almost anywhere as long as they are near an outside wall so the vent pipe has a place to go. You also have to have the space in your room to be sure the stove is safe with 9" of air space for the back and at least 3" for the sides. We were lucky...we had the room.

So how else did we get to putting in a pellet stove? Well you see my wife and I have always wanted to build a log home here in Vermont but for some reason that just hasn't even become our reality and we are pretty sure that it isn't going to happen anytime real soon. So when we needed to do some work to finish up our family room so it could be used as a bedroom temporarily, "Guess What?" we decided to finish it off using knotty pine paneling, pine trim and accessories just like a log home. It's kind of a log home in a tri-level house concept. It's not perfect or totally complete but it is our little piece of log cabin life in the Green Mountains of Vermont.

Talking about log homes...today, after church, we are headed off to visit Sheila and Mike, two of our friends that own a huge maple sugaring operation and live in – you guessed it – a log home. I remember asking Sheila at one time how she liked living in a log home and she replied rather quickly ... "Well you do know that this one is new and is a log home just like our last one." That was a pretty good indication to me that both she and Mike like them.

It's always fun to go and visit them, especially this time of year being winter and all. They built their house on a piece of property that originally was just the home of their sugarhouse and a whole bunch of trees, foliage and other things you would expect to find in the woods. It is built on top of a hill that has a pretty steep climb. During the winter, depending on which of the vehicles I choose to take, I can usually get to the first level spot on their driveway without any trouble and can usually make it to the next level spot which is where the sugarhouse sits today ... but sometimes getting to the next place, their house is a bit more of a challenge and often we end up parking at the sugarhouse and walking the rest of the way up to the house. But I have to tell you that just like a lot of the other things we talk about in our "On Vermont Time..." stories, getting all the way up the hill is definitely worth it.

You see just as soon as you start to head up their driveway you begin a journey that is out of this world. In true Vermont fashion, the cares of the world slow down and seem to disappear if only for a short time. Time stands still while you are there. You are close enough to the reality and the sounds of population but far enough away to be able to relax from the grind of living in it.

Don't forget I wrote that our friends are maple sugar makers. In fact, their company name is Rocky Ridge Sugar Makers to be exact. They sell some of the best maple syrup, maple candy and one my favorite's maple crème. That's what Kathy and I plan on buying today … a little plastic tub of it to take home and spread over toast with tomorrow's breakfast. Umm… Umm… Good.

But you know you just can't stop by their place, run in and buy something and then just run off. There is no fun in that. You have to stop long enough to be able to comb through all the Vermont Handmade Crafts, Gifts, Books, Photos and Food goodies that Sheila has in the shop. There are even a few of my gospel CDs on the shelf. You cannot help but love this place. There are always goodies to eat, some coffee to drink, and some stories to share – who knows, some of those stories just might show up here. Well we've told those stories long enough that the dark of the Vermont night has settled in and the moonlight is starting to grow brighter. It's time to head home. We have had a great, relaxing day, good times, good food, and good friends, all "On Vermont Time…"

Rocks

Poetry by Roderick Bates

When the glacier came down from Canada and sculpted our scarred valleys, it brought with it stones, boulders, pebbles. And when the great ice melted, the rocks settled, strewn as they now are, on the land, and in it. And each spring the frost propels another batch upward, our primal crop, the one that never fails, that does not fall to pests or blight or sudden storm. And the joke is told:

Where did all these rocks come from?
Glacier brung 'em.
Where's the glacier?
Gone back for more.

But there is another story, weighty as ledge, more pointed than broken slate: Forever the yearly pulse of freeze and thaw has sifted them upward, as the flecks of gold emerge from the panner's gentle swirl, and forever they have stuck in a hidden web as virgin cedar and maple and oak spread their tangled roots into a vast net against which the rocks press and pile, held through the centuries, bumping against an ever-growing ceiling until the white settlers cleared the forests, and slowly the roots died and broke up, and in a sudden rush that great jam loosened and rose, bobbing to the surface wave after wave, year after year. And the true answer arises with them, lifting into visibility from the darkness of our ignorance:

Where did all these rocks come from?
Truth be told, we brung 'em on ourselves.

Chapter 3

Slide for Life

By Lou Hill

A recent snowstorm left a blanket of snow on the steep hill outside my house, and jarred a few of the memory cells that still function in my brain. It brought back some of my experiences on Enosburg's winter roads back when I was young and extremely foolish.

In those days Buster and Lil Garrett lived next door to my grandmother, Ada Hill. I could usually be found over at their house playing with their daughter, Avis. Actually I tried to keep up with Avis, as even then, she was a very determined leader.

One of the Garrett family's prized possessions was a travois sled. To those of you who are unfamiliar with a travois, let me explain. A travois is a homemade version of a bobsled crossed with a luge, but with none of the refinements and certainly none of the safety features of either. It was made from a large 2 x 12, about eight feet long. The travois had a set of fixed steel runners in back with a second set of runners in front. The whole contraption could be steered with an old automobile steering wheel. There was no front nose for streamlining or protection, no handholds ...and no brakes.

Since the travois had narrow steel runners and considerable weight when loaded with five or six kids, it sank into the loose snow like a milk truck in mud season. So, to make it go, we needed to find a smooth, icy run like the ones used by bobsledders. The closest we could get in Enosburg were the back

11

roads. Fortunately, the ideal road was close by: the old Center Road, which gave us a run of about a mile. And, since a plowed back road would become hard-packed and quite slippery after very little traffic, it made a perfect run.

A group of us including Avis, some of the Corron and LaCross kids, and Avis' ever-present canine companion, Freckles, would drag the sled up past the Grange Hall to the top of the hill. At the top, we would all pile on. Avis would usually steer. She was fearless and, besides, it was her travois. I would get stuck in the middle since I was the smallest and the most scared. One of the bigger kids would push us off. By the time we negotiated the corner by the Grange Hall, we would have built up a pretty good head of steam. To me it always seemed supersonic, but it really wasn't all that fast as gravel and stones had usually worked up through the hard-packed snow and provided enough friction to slow us down. Also, some of the chicken-hearted (usually me) would drag our feet. If we were still going too fast as we approached the main road, we would either ram into a snowbank or tip the sled. Fortunately we never broke our necks or other important bones, and we always seemed to stop before we slid out into the main road.

Alas, I haven't seen a travois in years. But I have seen another type of suicide machine that we use to play with as kids. We called them "skooters," but they had several different names such as "ski jack" or "jack-jumpers." Avis' father made her one by nailing a seat made of 2 x 4's onto an old barrel stave. Skooters required a good sense of balance, lots of loose snow, a steep hill, and no brains. They were steered by leaning and luck.

Some of the more adept riders could make runs from top to bottom without falling off. Needless to say, I rarely made runs longer than ten feet, usually wiping out in a cloud of snow. The accepted method of stopping a skooter was falling off or running into a large immoveable object. Since we were using them in loose snow, there was little danger of doing permanent danger to ourselves,

While I managed to survive the travois and the skooter with little damage, Wendall Corron and I left some of our young hides on the blacktop when we slid down the Center Road hill on his Flexible Flyer. I was in my early teems by this time; older but no smarter. We used to drag Wendall's sled to the top of the hill to make our run. Wendall would lie down on the sled. I would push us off and then plop down on top of him. Fortunately, he is from hardy stock and my bulk crashing down on him didn't impair his steering ability too much. By this time (the early 1950's) the main road had been paved and was heavily salted during the snowstorms so that it was usually bare macadam. We would come rocketing off the side road onto the main road. The natural laws of physics dictated that when the steel runners hit pavement, they stopped. Unfortunately, our bodies usually didn't stop!

One night we almost lost our whole hides on that road. It had been snowing pretty steadily and the town plows had been out since early afternoon. The back road was in perfect shape for sliding; the plow had been through several times and the blade had packed the snow. Since there had been little or no traffic and the stones hadn't worked up through the snow, we had nothing to slow us down. We pushed off as usual and slued around the Grange Hall corner faster than a turpentined dog.

As we came down the straightaway to the end of the run, I looked up and saw one of the town plows passing my grandmother's house and head in our direction. Wendall spotted the truck at the same time, but instead of steering us out into the middle of the main road as he usually did, he managed to hug the edge of the road. They say God protects fools and little children, and you can decide for yourself which category we fit into. The scowling driver sped past us with a blast of his horn. As we slowed to a stop, we collapsed in gales of laughter triggered by relief or exhilaration – or probably both. Then we trudged back up that hill.

A Little Bit of History ... On Vermont Time

This is a photo of the Guy Green Family Farm and Sawmill
in West Enosburg as it looked in 1954 *(Photo courtesy of Harold Green)*

This is a photo of Enosburg's Main Street Businesses destroyed by a major
fire in 2005. The brick building to the left still stands today. The others have
been rebuilt into a beautiful new Main Street. *(Photo courtesy of Joanne Stetson)*

Chapter 4

Cats

By Lou Hill

My family have always been cat lovers. One of my favorite pictures of my mother shows her and my Uncle Jimmy each holding a huge cat, wide grins on their faces. My Aunt Doris stands between them, scowling, probably waiting for a cat fight to erupt.

My wife, Gwen, and I are currently owned by two cats, a calico and a tiger and white devil. The calico is named Cali, for her color, and the tiger is Tinker, short for Tinkerbell, because she flits from spot to spot.

Tinker is my cat. I found her in a blackberry patch up back a few years ago. She rode to Long Island with us, perched on my shoulder, one of her favorite spots. She will jump to my shoulder at the most unexpected moments. This frequently happens when I am enthroned in the bathroom, my favorite reading spot. She will leap to my shoulder and curl up around my neck, settling there, purring in my ear, until I get a stiff neck and shrug her off.

We have never been original with names. Most of our tiger cats have been named Timmy, a name originated by my mother for our first cat and continued with little regard for sex.

Several years ago, when we lived down in Bristol, we had Timmy IV. One of our neighbors had a mischievous little tiger kitten named Bambi who was a frequent visitor at our house. Bambi's mistress had a liking for strong drink and frequently forgot to feed him. Bambi would get disgusted and move to our house for a few days. My wife is a sucker for waifs.

One bitter cold winter day I opened the back door to find Bambi on the back steps. I wouldn't let him in as the rest of the family was still asleep. The two cats would tear around and lay waste to the house, if left unwatched. I went on out to water the horse and pony, following a path I had shoveled in the deep snow. I stayed out with the animals for several minutes. As I started back to the house, I met Bambi on his way home. He stalked down the path, never looking left or right. As he passed me, mumbling to himself in cat talk, I swear that he called me a SOB. A few weeks later Bambi moved in with us permanently.

Of all our cats, my favorite was Timmy II. This particular Timmy was a little bob-tailed female, a gray and black tiger. We got her when I was about ten years old. At the time we lived in the big three-rent apartment house on the end of Orchard Street.

The house had flat-roofed porches both in front and in back. My mother was a firm believer in fresh air while you slept, so our bedroom windows were always open, winter and summer. Since we didn't have screens, the open windows let Timmy come and go as she wished.

Like most cats, Timmy's favorite time to prowl was at night. She always slept with me and would go to bed when I did. When she got the hunting urge she would leave through her private exit. When she had enough, she would climb back up the tree, come in through my bedroom window and curl up on my bed. Since I sleep like the dead and won't wake up unless a bomb explodes under my bed, she never disturbed me.

One night Timmy apparently played with a skunk on one of her nocturnal expeditions with the usual results. My mother often told me about waking up and smelling this horrible odor. She went into my bedroom and there I lay; flat on my back, mouth open, sleeping blissfully away with an unhappy little cat, reeking of skunk, curled up on my chest.

Timmy's most memorable exploit occurred on a hot summer night when I was about eleven. Apparently Timmy got the hunting urge and wandered down to her favorite hunting spot, Titus Brook. After capturing a small green frog, she decided to bring it home to her family. Rather than come in my window as she usually did, she climbed the tree by the front porch and went in the window to my parent's bedroom.

Because of the hot weather, my mother had on a thin rayon nightgown and was sleeping without sheets. Timmy hopped up on the bed and deposited a wet, still squirming frog smack on my mother's stomach. The resulting scream even woke me up. We got screens shortly after that.

At this moment there is a tiger and white ball of fluff perched on my shoulder who seems to be asking, "What do you mean your favorite cat? Who are you talking about if you don't mean me?" Sorry about that, Tinker.

Covered Bridges ... On Vermont Time

This is a photo of the Hopkins Bridge spanning the Trout River originally built in 1875 by Sheldon and Savannah Jewett. *(Photo by Gardner Stetson, courtesy of Joanne Stetson)*

This is the Fuller Bridge spanning the Black Falls Brook in Montgomery. Built by the Jewett Bros. in 1890. *(Photo by Gardner Stetson, Courtesy of Joanne Stetson)*

Chapter 5

"First Summertime Camping Trip of 2006" "On Vermont Time…"

By Timothy G. Stetson

Day 1 – The first night – Thursday, July 6th

It is nighttime in a back woods camping area in northern Vermont, Brookside Campground in Enosburg Center, to be exact. It is a place to get away from the grind of a fast everyday life and relax with nature all around. My pagers will work but unfortunately, or fortunately I guess is the correct term, my cell phone does not work. If an emergency arises I will have to drive five miles down the road to get a signal but here's hoping that nothing comes up.

The campground itself has been built over the last few years by a man and his wife who own the land that it now sits on. He retired from working for the state and now spends most of his time working on his current pet project, the campground. He has built it site by site and between those of us that come here for weekends and those that have semi-permanent sites for the entire summer, the place stays pretty busy all season long. It is a great place to visit and to stay if you are looking for a fun Vermont camping experience. It is one of many camping attractions in our great state but is the one that I will focus on for this segment of our series.

Our home for the weekend is Site 44. My wife and I have just returned from sitting with my sister, brother-in-law and their 3 children next to the campfire on their site. Our youngest son has just driven back to the village to stay at our home. He plans to return tomorrow afternoon after he finishes some work that he needs to do for his landscaping customers.

The sparks from the fire make their way up into the tree line and then disappear into the night sky. As we look up we can see the faint outline of the clouds but so far no rain and luckily none is predicted for the entire weekend. It is a time to sit and tell stories and everyone has one even the youngest of the children. They each take turns telling stories about each other and this really inspires us as adults to do the same. It is great to reminisce under the nighttime sky.

And what fun is relaxing and storytelling if you don't have snacks to go along with it. And what is the best campfire snack in the whole world? Well s'mores of course. Ummm Ummm Good. Put a marshmallow on a stick, hold it over the campfire not too close or not too far away, get it nice and golden brown without burning it, add a piece of Hershey's chocolate bar, put the marshmallow and the chocolate bar piece between two graham crackers and viola you have a s'more. They are so yummy that of course you want s'more. Just have to be careful you don't eat too many – don't want a belly ache.

The brook is not too high right now. It seems to be running at pretty normal levels which is a really exciting concept because this summer here in the Green Mountains of Vermont we have not had many days or nights without rain. Lord knows we don't want Brookside Campground to turn into Raging River Campground while we are here. Talking about the brook, we can hear the water cascading over the rocks below just outside our camper; it is very relaxing to go to sleep to. The smoothness of the sound plays a tune of solitude. Nature sounds therapy at its best. Many people pay good money for recordings of the sounds that we hear just outside our door.

Not only do we have the soothing sound of water but we also have some local wildlife to keep us interested. My sister saw a skunk that was probably making his rounds of all the campsites to see what great food all the humans have left for him tonight. Hopefully one of us will not bump into him in the night unexpectedly. I am not sure who will be more surprised, him or us. It will be a toss up to be sure. Some of the people that we know that stay at the campground all summer were talking about being able to hear a couple of bears over the last few weeks so you never know, we might get to see them too, where else but here in Vermont. It is this beauty of nature that sometimes I have to remind myself of when people say to me "Oh you live in Vermont? It is so beautiful there." Yes, it definitely is beautiful here and this is one of the best examples of that beauty.

Day 2 – The Next Morning – Friday, July 7th

The birds are chirping, a light breeze is whistling through the trees, the voices of children playing are heard and the smell of Green Mountain Coffee - Our Blend is wafting through the camper. It is Friday morning at the campground and the sunshine illuminates the natural beauty of the landscape around us. Oh what a beautiful day!

It is sponge bath time just before putting on the eggs and sausage that are a staple of our family camping trips. My mother's adage is that there is never any excuse for not being clean. "You can take a bath with a teaspoon of water if you plan it right," She always says. Well luckily water and electricity are part of the amenities that come with each site here at Brookside, so we won't have to test her theory and we will smell and feel good to boot. For those though that like to rough it, you don't have to use the amenities, you can pitch your tent and experience the great outdoors to the fullest.

My sister's daughters are already grabbing their bicycles to go riding on the winding roads that make up the campground. They can just ride around or go up and play on the swings, slides and teeter totters that make up the play area. They never stay in one place too long. They are just excited to be at camp. Her oldest son has been whittling all morning. He loves the outdoors and is very artistic and creative. Last night he brought over a comic book that he and a friend have created, drawn and written. It was really good and was interesting enough so I wanted to read through the whole thing. This morning he was looking for a little more intense whittling project and decided that he would whittle and carve a cross. I am sure I will be able to witness his handiwork here in a little while.

Oh boy! I can hear the crackling of the sausage patties on the hot pan. The smell of it cooking mixes with the scent of coffee and lo and behold it is morning time aromatic heaven. As my wife cooks the sausage and readies the eggs for the breakfast meal, I start preparing the toast and filling our coffee cups. She finishes the sausage and completes the scrambling of the eggs, we eat, relax, share time with each other and sit and do a little writing, and it is the start of another great day "On Vermont Time..."

Breakfast is done, the dishes are washed and now the kids are down by the brook digging up some natural clay. They want to make handprints. It is cheaper than running to the craft store, that's for sure.

Now it's time to go and take some photos of the picturesque landscape that surrounds us. There is green everywhere you look and with the extra color presented by the wild flowers and plants you are sure to fill an album with views that will delight anyone who looks through it.

Day 2 – Afternoon and Evening

My sister's son is out looking for a better piece of whittlin' wood for his cross project. The pieces he has found up to now don't seem to do the trick. Just as he heads out screams emanate from the brook side as one of his sisters loses her grasp on the little pail she is playing with in the water. It starts to float away only to be saved by another of his sisters as she dives into the rushing water to rescue it. Now they're both wet from the tips of their toes up to their neckline but the pail is safe and back in the hands of its owner. Off he goes to do some more on his cross project. There is never much time to rest for the budding artist.

The kids are picking on me because for about the fourth time today I have lost my pen. Just can't seem to keep it clipped to my shirt. I loaned it to my nephew for some of his project work but we both know he gave it back to me. Well it will either turn up or I will need to find a new one. The one I lost is from Bond Auto Parts, a family-owned full service parts company that has stores all over Vermont and New Hampshire. They have grown from being a one-store operation to a wholesale operation to now a complete turnkey company owned store network. It has been kind of fun to watch them develop. My oldest son works for them now and really seems to like it.

Most of the afternoon has been spent lazing around and relaxing, something I don't do very well but am working at. My oldest niece and my nephew are in and out of my wife's and my camper as they continue to put finishing touches on the little stories that they are writing on the laptop. I guess seeing their uncle work on this series has inspired them to want to do some writing themselves. My nephew wants to write a bestselling book and pay his own way through college. Time will tell whether he will be able to do it or not but knowing how he ticks I am guessing that he will figure out a way.

Talking about writers, Vermont is home or has become home for many authors that are found on bookshelves today. Some, of course, have lived here from birth but there are others that have moved here to get away from the hustle and bustle of city living so they can write without many distractions. One of my favorites is Archer Mayor who writes mystery novels. Joe Citro, who writes accounts of ghost stories and other legends, is also very well known around these parts. Another friend, Dick Harper writes a myriad of material and one friend, Lou Hill, who recently passed away, wrote articles about Vermont living and history just like I do. An example of those that have moved here or at least come to Vermont for the summer is Colleen Curran who not only is a writer of novels but is an award winning Canadian playwright as well. My wife and I are both very pleased to be able to call Colleen our friend. She is a bundle of energy and is just fun to be around.

Update on the cross carving project. My nephew has discovered that it is a little too difficult to whittle a cross without first being able to cut out the basic shape and then work on it so today's project has become a knife carving of a wooden knife or probably something closer to a machete.

Early evening has now set upon us; we have finished the suppertime meal of macaroni & cheese and ham steak and are preparing for the activities of the evening. We kind of expect our youngest son to come and visit and he will probably show up just about the time we have to head to Enosburg Center and then on to Richford. Lo and behold, I couldn't have known how right I would be. Now that it's time to run to the Enosburg Center Memorial Church where I pastor Summer Outreach Services of the Richford First Baptist Church on Sunday mornings, he is driving in. He brought Sophie our dog to see us and has agreed to hang around until we get back. We figure we will be gone about 2 hours.

Tonight we are meeting with a couple that is planning their wedding for late in August. The memorial church is a grand old building and a great place for a wedding. It is also serving us well for the summer church services we are holding. The church was originally built in 1827 and then rebuilt in 1876. It is built in the old wood frame tradition like many of the churches throughout Vermont. It, like many Vermont churches, is a two-story building with the sanctuary being on the top floor and the fellowship hall in the lower level with an entry level kind of in between the two. But it wasn't always that way. According to some of the members of the original church, the building was built as a one story building and then when the congregation decided that they would really like a fellowship hall, they jacked up the one-story building and added a lower level that became the fellowship hall.

It is a fabulous old building and you can almost hear the stories of history if you sit in the sanctuary at night with nothing going on. There are many interesting things rooted in history about the building that we love. The interior furnishings are all original; the pew cushions are even dated and numbered for the individual pews. Talking pews, the pews have a divider down the center. They are family pews. In fact we understand that you just never sat in another family's pew. It was unheard of. Some of the people that have been attending our summer services tell the stories of those church services of old. There is enough church history on the hill that I will probably do a totally separate edition of "On Vermont Time…" specifically about the center church and maybe some of the others like it.

After spending some time showing the soon-to-be-married couple around the building, it was time for my wife and I to head to the First Baptist Church of Richford to record the music that we need for our church service on Sunday. We have a fantastic keyboard player in our churches but unfortunately he can only be in one church at a time as our services overlap so he had to record the music that we use for our service ahead of time. Through a grant we were able to purchase a Yamaha Clarinova Piano that he is able to play and record on. It has been working fantastically for us and so far no one has complained about the music being recorded and not live. We have a couple of old time hymn sings planned for the end of this month and into next month and he will be featured live at both of those events. That way we can have the best of both worlds.

Later that day …

It's time now for the Franklin Cub Scouts rain gutter regatta. This year it will be a little different as we have this huge brook only a few feet from where we are all camping and we're not using rain gutters. If you have never seen a race of these little wooden sailboats, you just haven't seen "good time" racing. The scouts each have to build their own racing sailboat with as little help from the "adults" around the house as possible – though everyone knows that most fathers and mothers just can't keep their fingers off the project. Usually on a Saturday during the year each scout brings his racing boat to a special meeting where rain gutters are set up in long rows in the elementary school gymnasium or some large building of this type. The gutters are filled with water. The sailboat is placed at one end … each scout is in position…the fans fill every open space in the room … the tension mounts … out comes the green flag to start the race and they're off!

By now you are probably wondering … "How does a sailboat made out of a little piece of wood move from one end of the rain gutter to the other without any wind. Well, there's wind of course. Hmmmm…How? The wind for the sails is yup you guessed it young cubs scouts blowing on them with all they've got to see which of them will get their boat over the finish line first.

This year it is going to be even more fun than normal and the only reason the scouts will become breathless is because they have run up and down the length of the brook so many times. Have you ever tried running through all those slippery rocks. It can take quite a toll. But all in all it really is cool to see all of this young energy flitting around in the brook water like those water bugs that you see swimming in water holes all over the place. And each one of them is a winner in their own right. They have all taken the time to finish their boat. They have each come to this event to race. And together they have learned about fairness in competition and have also learned a little bit about the fact that often times, things like races are more easily won if you work together as a team. What more could be asked of a scouting event like this.

Well nighttime is once again starting to fall all around us. We'll each prepare our last evening meal of the camping trip, head off to bed, and then get up tomorrow morning to prepare to pull out and head back to reality. Kathy and I will pack up and then head to church for our morning service. Our youngest son Dan will be here to pick up the camper, take it home until the next trip. We all sure hope that you have enjoyed this weekend camping trip with us and that maybe, just maybe the day will come when you too can enjoy camping at one of our beautiful Vermont campgrounds ... maybe even Brookside ... "On Vermont Time..."

Chapter 6

"Another Autumn in Enosburg Falls"
"On Vermont Time..."

By Timothy G. Stetson

This story was the second one I ever wrote in this "On Vermont Time..." series of stories about the little Green Mountain Village of Enosburg Falls, Vermont. I wrote then: It seems funny to be writing again about fall but as I look back at my first "On Vermont Time" it was written in the fall of 2000. Here it is 2002 and this is just the next little entry in this journal. Enosburg Falls is tucked in the northern portion of the state, just 7 miles from the Canadian Border. I hope you find the time to come and visit our little village and spend a little while "On Vermont Time..." If you can't come to us...I hope these stories bring us a little closer to you and provide you with some relaxing enjoyment.

The sun is setting behind the mountains and hills filled with the reds and oranges of autumn. "I don't think they are as bright as last year but they sure are beautiful," says my wife Kathy while we stand there not only looking at the leaves but watching 2 flocks of geese flying over head making their annual trip to the south. "They're following the river," Kathy says, "Look at the small group trying to catch up with that big one." The continual squawking is a true sign of fall this time but also signifies spring earlier in the year.

It is autumn again here in little Enosburg Falls, Vermont. The corn fields are in varying states of harvest. Some are completely bare, some are half chopped and then others are still standing tall awaiting their turn of the harvesters. It is a kind of fun time of year here. The air is a little cooler, the sun is not out as much but there is still the smell and feeling of autumn in the air. It brings back the memories of jumping in a tall pile of leaves, something we used to do as kids. It is a little difficult to explain but very fun to experience.

Our sons David and Daniel and, of course, Kathy and I are currently working on preparations for the Annual Opera House Talent Search. The Talent Search, this year, is celebrating its 10th year. It has been fun to view the videos from the past ten years as we put together a multi-media collage that will be shown the night of the show. Oh...some of the acts from the past...you just have to laugh. This annual event though pulls out some of Northern Vermont's finest talent of all ages. If you ever have a chance to visit us during the fall season, usually the talent search is in October. It is a show that you don't want to miss.

Of course, I can't forget the annual Haunted Extravaganza that we work on. It features the Haunted Spavin Cure. This great old building... I have written about it before... was the home of the Dr. B.J. Kendall Company many years ago. They manufactured many products, one of which was Prof. Flint's Horse and Cattle Condition and Renovating Powders. We are going to manufacture 2 days of eerie haunting fun there. The whole town gets involved in one way or another. We have school kids and adults that have been helping us with building and, on the days of the 2 shows - oh yeah, this year we actually extended the event to 2 days because we had to turn 400 people away last year - will be the actors. There will be all kinds of other events around the village - a spooky activity room on Saturday, a haunted barn for the kids on Sunday, the pumpkin glow on the park on Saturday night and hay rides, bands, and refreshments. What's even better? A portion of the proceeds go to benefit the work of the Enosburgh Fire Department and Enosburgh Ambulance Service. Here again, is another great facet of living in a small Vermont town. We like to support each other and the services that serve our community.

There is much talk right now about the elections coming up. Our current Governor, Howard Dean is in his last month of office. He is currently doing all the legwork to make a run for President. Each of the parties this year has a strong candidate for Governor. It sure makes the race a little more fun than normal when you know that one party or the other doesn't have a "shoe in" for the slot. Elections in our little town are basically the same as they used to be and still use a paper ballot. The Board of Civil Authority, as it is known, will get together on election day and work throughout the day making sure that everyone who wants to has a chance to vote on paper ballots and then will take whatever time it takes after the polls close to count the ballots...a fun process.

What is the Board of Civil Authority, you say? Well it is made up of all of us Justices of the Peace. There are more than 1800 Justices of the Peace in Vermont making it the most numerous and popular public office in the state. It is among the oldest public offices and was first created by the Vermont Constitution of 1777. Justices are elected by the voters of their respective towns and serve as election officials, a responsibility that actually started in the mid-Nineteenth century, as well as hear tax abatement questions and appeals, administering oaths and acting as notary publics. Oh yes, we can solemnize weddings and civil unions. This part of our job was first established in 1779, but at that time the jurisdiction was limited to the county for which each justice was elected. In 1975 the jurisdiction was extended statewide. These are the real fun responsibilities of the job. Being a Justice of the Peace is a Vermont tradition. Thank you Secretary of State, Deborah Markowitz for the information described here from "The J.P. Guide" published in 2001.

Well I hope you have enjoyed reading some more about our little town, village, and the state in which they reside. I can hear Kathy calling "Tim, it's time for supper." So I must leave you now. I look forward to sharing more with you next time... "On Vermont Time..."

Landmarks ... On Vermont Time

Samsonville Power Dam Control Building

The Opera House at Enosburg Falls

Chapter 7

High Explosives

By Lou Hill

I used to like to blow things up. Not with any particular malicious intent. I wasn't looking to do any damage to anyone or to their property, I just liked explosions.

Wendell Corron, my oldest friend, and I started hanging out together when he was about 8 and I was 6. One of the things that I remember about those early days of our friendship was a big metal safe-like object located down in the back of his house. I soon learned that it was indeed an old safe. Many years before it had been used as a records vault when the Town of Enosburg, Vermont officers were at Enosburg Center.

When the Town Clerk's Office was moved from the Center to Enosburg Falls, the safe was moved to a spot in a field in back of the Corron's house next to Tyler Branch. It was used by the Town Highway Department as storage for DYNAMITE.

For years Wendell and I tried every imaginable way to break into that vault. If we had been successful, we had every intention of stealing some dynamite. Fortunately for all concerned, we never were. Every time we passed by that vault we tried the handles. Maybe, just maybe, someone had forgotten to lock it.

I remember one day when we thought that fortune had smiled down on us. We were on our way through the field to the fishing and swimming hole that we called "Two Streams." As we passed the vault we saw that one of the doors was ajar. We pulled both doors open and there in front of us were two heavy waxed cardboard boxes with the magic word printed on them – DYNAMITE.

We pawed madly through the boxes. Nothing! Empty! Visions of blowing up something, anything, faded. Never again would we come that close to our goal.

Wendell's grandfather, a veteran of the Spanish American War, lived near the Corrons. He still had the old government issue 45-70 rifle that he had carried in that campaign. One winter day, when we were in our early teens, he made Wendell a present of the rifle. Along with the rifle, he gave him half a dozen rounds of ammunition. They were loaded with black powder and were probably issued to him along with the rifle. The cartridges were huge and seemed like shells for a howitzer to Wendell and I, who were used to shooting a .22.

Naturally we couldn't wait to fire the old rifle. We hurried back to the Corron's house and went down by their garage. Wendell opened the breech, it was a rolling block, and loaded it with one of those monster shells. The gun was massive. It must have weighed well over twelve pounds and been nearly five feet long. In order to steady it, Wendell leaned the gun up against the corner of the garage.

I peered over Wendell's shoulder, so anxious to see what was going on that I was practically in his back pocket. Wendell cocked the rifle and squeezed off a shot. The resulting explosion and concussion shook the garage so much that all the snow on the roof cascaded down on top of us.

Wendell's father, Fred, raced out of the house. When he got outside he was met by the sight of a cloud of foul smelling smoke and two laughing boys covered in snow. He quickly collared us, positive that we had finally succeeded in breaking into the vault and getting our hands on some dynamite.

When he realized his error, we caught the what-for because we had fired the old gun without his permission.

Since we couldn't steal dynamite we decided to do the next best thing manufacture our own. Somewhere one of us found a formula for mixing black powder. For obvious reasons I won't reveal it here. Suffice it to say that the ingredients were fairly easy for us to obtain.

We also picked up the information that, to insure a good even mixture, the ingredients should be mixed with water, and then dried out. We proceeded to combine the chemicals and water coming up with a black, soupy mess. Not being the most patient individuals, we decided to speed up the drying process.

At the time, it seemed like a bright idea to place the concoction in a pan in the oven of the Corron's wood stove to dry it out. It worked like a charm, too. Why we didn't blow up the stove and ourselves along with it is beyond me. Wendell and I seemed to have a very efficient guardian angel looking after us in those days.

Unfortunately, or perhaps fortunately, our homemade explosive never did work too well. We were never able to obtain any impressive blasts. All we ever got from our detonations were some flashes and sulfurous smelling smoke.

I finally did attain my goal of blowing something up. It happened on the Enosburg/Bakersfield town line. The construction crew was blasting some of the narrow old cement bridges prior to putting in forms for new bridges. I happened to come along just at the time when the man was blasting was ready to blow the bridge.

"Hey Kid. You want to set off the charge?"

Was George Aiken a Republican? With trembling hands, I took the generator and pushed down the T-handle. Kawhump! Small chunks of concrete rained down on us. There wasn't the concern for safety in those days, and blasting mats and hard hats were rarely used. But even if I had gotten a concussion – who cared? I had finally blown up something.

Winter in Vermont

Poetry by Lauren L. Young

From the sky above, they drift down
A wet feathery mass falling, falling, falling
Embellishing us with the season's garb
The streetlights reflect glistening white gems
As they blanket rooftops, vehicles
And the earth's surroundings.

Oh, towering tree, how majestic you are tonight,
Your once naked-grey limbs bow in their new
stylish coats.
I blink as a snowflake strikes my eyelash.
Others land on my floppy hat, furry coat
And knee-high boots.
Soon I am a cake-frosted figure.
Slipping and sliding down the snow-covered street.

Tomorrow children clad in cold weather gear
Will squeal with delight
As they frolic in the snow
Hurling snowballs to and fro.
Snowmen and various snow sculptures
will dot our yard.
We will ski, snowmobile, shovel, shiver,
Complain and enjoy.
Ah yes, once again, it's "Winter in Vermont!"

Chapter 8

Duffy's Army

By Lou Hill

In the next few years many events of World War II will be commemorated. However, the exploits of one of the oddest outfits in the annals of military history will remain unnoticed. This group was made up of individuals wearing an assortment of uniforms from all branches of the service...A ragtag band willing to follow their leader anywhere.

Sounds like something similar to the *Dirty Dozen* or *The Guns of Navarone*, doesn't it? In reality this group more closely resembled *The Little Rascals* meet Abbott and Costello in *Buck Privates*. Their theater of action was here in a Vermont jungle behind Tunk Burleson's Mobil station in the center of Enosburg Falls, with an occasional foray to the banks of the Missisquoi River.

The army was made up of a group of a dozen or so 8 to 14 year olds. Most of the activity took place during the summer months from 1943 to 1945. The requirements of the school calendar mandated cessation of hostilities during the rest of the year. Our fearless leader was Tommy Duffy, who had assumed this position as his right. He was the oldest of the group, and he supplied most of our armament. The loft behind his father's store provided our headquarters and served as our barracks, planning room or transport plane depending on the particular scenario of the day.

Many members of the army had colorful nicknames including, among others, Peanut Kennison, second in command; Wimpy Sweeny; and Stinky Stanley. My nickname came at the time when I had somewhat of an identity problem. My father's family called me by my baptismal name of Louis or quite frequently Louis James (never Lou or Louie) while my mother's family preferred Billy. This confusion was solved when Duffy tagged me with the name Jellybean.

Uniforms were an interesting conglomeration of patches, insignia and stripes, with an occasional authentic article of clothing from every branch of the service. Almost every member of our army had a close relative in some branch of the military. Most painfully scrawled letters to them included a request for one of these items.

Many of our missions required us to parachute into enemy territory. The loft that functioned as our airborne troop transport had a wide door approximately eight to ten feet above the ground. It was a perfect jumping off site. To a myopic, overweight, and less than athletic eight year old, it was also an intimidating distance. I did make a few jumps thus earning the acceptance of my peers. However I usually weaseled out by volunteering to act as pilot of our aircraft. This allowed me to babble on about approaching enemy fighters, or to announce the upcoming drop zone or whatever else came to mind based on the number of war comic books or movies I had seen recently. It also let me avoid making those terrifying jumps which the other troops seemed to anticipate with great glee. They would leap from the open door with screams of, "Geronimo," and land in a pile of soft sand. As I recall, Stinky Stanley usually acted as my co-pilot. I don't think he had any more stomach for the jumps than I did.

Parachutes were rolls of material wrapped with a cord that was attached to a static line prior to jumping out of the door. It was of paramount importance to remember to quickly roll out of the way after landing in the sand. Otherwise the next member of the group would land in the middle of your back or stomach.

We also fought many jungle campaigns. Our theaters of action seemed to shift from Europe to the Pacific with little regard for the logistics of troop movements. I always looked forward to the jungle engagements. It wasn't necessary to make a jump and I excelled at rooting around in the thick underbrush behind the Mobil station. In reality our jungle was a 200-foot square area of scrub trees and sumac. To us it was thick tropical undergrowth filled with all kinds of exotic animals, insects, snakes, and of course, the enemy.

Unfortunately, I suffered my only "wounds" of my military career during one of those jungle campaigns, a severe case of "red rump" which may have been poison ivy or some allergy to the plant life growing in the jungle. Fortunately it responded to the calamine treatments administered by Nurse Mom. In fact, my mysterious rash was about the only real medical emergency suffered by any of the troops. That in itself is remarkable, considering the duration and intensity of our activities.

One of my vivid memories of the jungle was a mountain of empty quart oil cans piled up behind the station. Since this pile was the highest point around, it had significant tactical value. Many of our missions required scaling the heights of "Oil Can Mountain" to establish a lookout post. There was still a little oil remaining in the cans, even though they had been drained in a special rack after being used by the garage. We would end up with liberal coatings of oil all over us after a few minutes of mock battle. This did not endear us with our mothers.

On occasion we made longer treks down to the banks of the Missisquoi River and to Central Vermont's railroad trestle spanning a small brook. There we would either blow up the trestle for the umpteenth time, or engage an enemy force led by Cookie LaFlamme, another local boy who had formed his own troop of fighting men.

We also made forays to the point of land extending into the river below the local Electric Light Department's dam. This area was off-limits to most of us by parental order, and to all of us by order of the Light Department. Consequently this was a mission that fell into the "Top Secret" classification. Usually these missions deteriorated into a search for fool's gold, which was rumored to be in the area. As hard as I searched, I never found any.

Eventually all wars must end, even play wars. Ours was no exception. The entry of the world into the Atomic Age brought an end to World War II as well as our own. For Tommy and some of the older boys, it signaled the end of youth.

Some of us complained because we wouldn't have a chance to really fight Japs and Nazis. Little did we know that there would be other wars and other chances to fight in places that we had never heard of at that time. Places like Korea and Vietnam.

Chapter 9

Straightening Nails

By Roderick Bates

Here in New England we are very conscious of our heritage. Some of this is superficial, like putting the construction dates of our houses in big numerals over the front door or bragging about how many generations of Vermont (or New Hampshire or Rhode Island) ancestors we have. Some of it, though, is more meaningful.

My father believed that one element of his Vermont heritage was an obligation to pass along a set of values to me. Much of this he accomplished verbally, but often what he said was only part of what he was passing along.

When I was quite young my Dad helped a friend remove a several-room wooden addition from the back of a brick house. His pay was all of the lumber he could haul away. Dad and I pulled nails out of boards and beams, and Dad stacked the lumber behind the garage. He used most of it over the next three or four years in a variety of projects, including adding a two-story addition to our own home.

Under Dad's careful eye I learned how to pull nails without damaging the wood they were embedded in. In almost all cases, the nails protruded through the back of the board. Some were bent over in the board to insure that they would not work loose. Working from the back of the board, I would pry any bent-over nails up straight, then gently pound the tips of the nails with the hammer, driving them partially out of the board.

Then I could flip the board and get the claws of the hammer under the heads of the nails and pry them out. For long nails, a small piece of two-by-four between the hammer and the board allowed an extra pull. When a board was completely free of nails, it could be added to the stack of lumber.

Next, the nails were sorted by size and put in coffee cans. My grandfather, a cigar smoker, had stored all of his nails in cigar boxes. To this day, I have in my workshop a stack of neatly labeled White Owl boxes, arrayed beside the Maxwell House cans my father used.

When all of the good nails were sorted we were left with a tangled pile of bent nails.

Dad then got a hammer and a flat rock. "Come here, Son," he said, "let me show you how to straighten nails. You can help me a lot if you do this."

He showed me how to roll a nail on the rock until the nail humped up, then tap it with a hammer to flatten out the hump. Sometimes the nail would roll when struck, pinching my fingers, and I would have to try again. Sometimes I would have to turn the nail several times to get all of its humps pounded down, each turn bringing the nail a little closer to straight.

"Nails cost money, Son," Dad explained, "there's no need to spend money when you can use what you already have."

When I would tire of straightening nails I would put the ones I had straightened in the proper cans. There were always more bent nails for me to tackle the next time I was helping my Dad with his carpentry.

As I got older, I began to work on projects by myself, building little ramps for my toy trucks to go over, or boxes to hold my marbles.

Once, one glorious Spring when I was 10 or 11, I built a raft, slicing my hand open when a hand saw (hence the name?) flexed and leapt out at me. I launched the raft in the Williams River, lost my balance and nearly drowned. I still have scars from the construction and memories of my Mother's concern when I dragged home, soaked and muddy, bandages swept off in the current, blood running down my hand and mixing with the mud on my fingers.

As I worked more with wood, I discovered that bent nails weren't such a great thing to work with. Once bent, they had a tendency to bend again when you pounded them. I would find myself making fairly complex calculations in applied physics, just to hit a warped nail on the side I thought would keep it from bending and actually drive it into the wood. With practice, and with great patience and light taps with the hammer, I learned to use straightened nails. But the more I used them, the less sense it made.

I was pretty sure that I understood the lesson of my Vermont heritage:

Vermonters are a frugal lot. They have to be; money is hard to come by on the sidehill farms that dot the landscape. Farm folks save, they reuse, they improvise and they get by.

In fact, the nails used to build a settler's house in the late 1700s might well have been the most costly items in its construction. The wood was all taken from the land. The labor was provided by the landowner and his sons. But the nails had to be purchased. When a farmhouse or barn burned, the settlers would sift through the ashes to find the nails and re-use them.

I knew all this. I respected it. But there didn't seem to be a core of sense to it all, at least not anymore. It was completely reasonable to reuse lumber, and since you had to pull the old nails out anyway, saving the good ones was just common sense. But straightening the bent ones? I could buy a pound of nails for 50 cents, and save a half hour of time. Even at minimum wage, my time was worth more than the 50 cents I spent on nails. So, I stopped straightening nails, and came to the conclusion that Dad had hung on to the old ways a little too long.

Then I married and had a daughter. Elizabeth: blond hair and blue eyes, running along on sturdy little legs, keeping up with Daddy as he headed for the workbench. Elizabeth, chattering away about everything, asking hundreds of questions: "What are you doing, Daddy? Can I help? What is this? How do you use it? What can I do? Is this how you hammer things?"

And I heard my Father's voice come out of my mouth. "Come here, Liz, let me show you how to straighten nails. You can help me a lot if you do this."

And the lesson shifted before my eyes: *Getting a job done with a child along is about five times as hard as it would be otherwise. Getting the work done involves keeping the child out from underfoot. Finding a project to occupy a child is part of the job.*

Initially, I felt tricked by my Dad. He hadn't wanted those damn nails; he just wanted me busy so he could get something done. I had banged away on countless nails for nothing, and wasted hours of time. For all I knew, he never used one of them.

Even as I showed my daughter how to straighten out nails, I was feeling like a trickster. I felt a mixture of amused surprise and anger: Dad had played a joke on me, and it wasn't until 30 years later that I had gotten it. But I had to concede that his approach was sound -- my daughter was falling for it just as thoroughly as I had.

Then I watched Elizabeth. She was concentrating on holding a nail just right, and was tapping it with her hammer. She was totally absorbed in her project, working with her Daddy.

Again the lesson shifted: *Raising a child is a complex honor.* Finally, I saw, as I watched my daughter bent over a flat rock, intently rolling nails and tapping them with a hammer, that the lesson wasn't really about economy. It was about spending time with your child and still getting your task done. It was about teaching your child to feel productive, and to contribute to the project at hand.

Oh, it gave Dad a chance to talk about being frugal, and in fact the lesson was learned. But really, the whole thing was about being a loving father in the real world. And that's a lesson beyond price.

Chapter 10

My Beloved Mother

By Lauren L. Young

Amid the flurry of the holiday season, I struggle with a tremendous sadness that each of us has to come to terms with when our parents are no longer with us. I take that aching loss, and I cruise down memory lane thankful for the warm memories that will forever reside in my heart, especially at Christmas Time.

My mom was a very clever lady. Her homemade delectable delights satisfied the palates of many. She was adept at sewing, and in her later years, she mastered the art of upholstery. Today, you will find her work throughout Franklin County.

Once when my three tiny urchins and I were visiting with mom, I had grown impatient with them. Mom took me by the hand and led me to the stairway.

"Be patient, Lauren," she said, "In a wink of an eye, they will be grown up and on their own."

Together, we perused the seven pictures on the wall. My picture being #6 followed by my only brother, David #7. A round baby face stared back at me.

"Why am I the only baby picture?" I asked.

Chuckling mom replied, "I was afraid the good Lord wouldn't give me six daughters and have them all sane and healthy." (debatable by some)

How we hooted!

Today my children are grown up and cruising down their life's path. With a great amount of pride, I watch my Stephanie teach her twenty month old son, Ian, through playing and nurturing. I tell her, "Be patient. In the wink of an eye he will be grown up and on his own."

Love and nurturing are the greatest gifts we can give our offspring. If your childhood memories were not happy ones, through choice, you have the opportunity to overcome your fear and anger and give the gift of unconditional love to your children; not just at Christmas, but all year long.

I look around my house, and the holiday spirit springs forth. The scent of pine needles tickles my nostrils. Christmas notes fill the air. I gaze underneath the Christmas tree at the miniature lighted manger scene, which long ago first brought a gleam to my eyes. On the mantel sits a picture of a precious snowman. My mom made him out of soap flakes. She also made his accessories. I run my finger over the picture and warm memories of a very kind lady with a big heart flow through me. She gave me unconditional love, and taught me what, "being," is all about. I wipe the tears from my face, and I count my blessings.

"Childhood Memories," is one of my tributes to, Mary, my beloved mom.

Chapter 11

December Journey to Stowe

By Timothy G. Stetson

It's a Winter Wonderland outside. I know you're thinking; "Now that isn't new for Vermont is it?" But it does seem to be really new for this year. I think we have to run to the record books to check but it must be some sort of record, almost no snow until the 7th of December. Well we got a little yesterday and then this morning we had 1.5" of the sparkling, frozen, white stuff on the back deck of our house when I went out to measure it.

Yuck, I am thinking – not only do I have to drive to Burlington in it but today I am taking a journey to Stowe. Sometimes as much as I love the beauty of Vermont – and I really, really do – I think I am getting old 'cause I just don't seem to like driving in the stuff like I used to. I mean I used to pray for snow in May and June so I could race around on my snow machine. But now that my snow machine is a Toyota Corolla, and I drive a minimum of 100 miles a day, I guess I don't like racing around in it quite so much.

But … then it hits me … Stowe, that's not so bad is it. First of all its not all that far from home or from Burlington – though it is a little farther to drive this time of year than the rest because "The Notch" as it's fondly called over Mount Mansfield is closed for the winter season. "Notch?" you say, "What is a notch?" We have a few of them in Vermont. The one I am talking about here is called Smuggler's Notch.

The Vermont State Parks website tells us that the now famous Smuggler's Notch is a narrow pass through the Green Mountains. It is a narrow road lined with 1,000-foot cliffs that is closed in winter. In its earlier days it was only a footpath and a trail for horses.

Why "Smuggler's?" … In 1807, President Thomas Jefferson passed an embargo act forbidding American trade with Great Britain and Canada. This as you can imagine created some real hardship for folks in northern Vermont since they were really close to Montreal. So to deal with the hardship, many locals continued the illegal trading with Canada by herding cattle and carrying other goods through the notch. Later, fugitive slaves used the Notch as an escape route to Canada and yes, there's more …. During the Prohibition years, liquor was smuggled to Canada over the improved road built in 1922.

Today, at least during the spring, summer, and fall many of us use the road as the quick route from Jeffersonville (Yup, you guessed it – named for President Thomas Jefferson) to Stowe. Believe it or not, it actually cuts at least 30 minutes off the trip from Enosburg Falls to Stowe. And of course the ride through the notch is a beautiful one with relaxing crystal springs, sparkling water falls, sleek rock faces and hiking trails galore. There are a number of scenic view pull offs on the trip through the mountain shoulder and if you are a spelunker there are numerous caves and caverns carved into the mountain walls to be explored.

On the ride, the closer you get to the top, the narrower the road gets and when you get to the point where you're about to "cut through the pass" the road turns into one lane, starts making sharp turns first left, then right, then left again and the rocks seem to spring up and get closer to your car. You definitely don't want to drive anything too large through there or you may leave parts of it right on top. Over the years a trucker or two has attempted the jaunt through the notch with macho trucker enthusiasm right up until they found themselves and their truck wedged between the rock unable to move one way or another, forward or back.

But enough about the notch; my second thought about the trip to Stowe is that it is just a great place to get away from the day to day cares of the everyday world. You can picnic, go to the spa, see theater productions, visit the Vermont Ski Museum, participate in one of the many events that are held every year throughout the community or just sit and feel the sun warming your face and the cool mountain breeze blowing through your hair. Ah yes, if you love winter sports and it is winter like right now you can ski, snowboard, snowmobile, hike and more all in the same place.

And we can't forget that there are also many great places to eat and not one of them is a McDonalds. Stowe had one for a short time but it wasn't long before it was "Out of Business." It was just no competition for all the other great eateries. Makes you kind of wonder ... is Stowe the only place a McDonalds has ever gone out of business. That'll be a research project for another writing I am sure.

As I start my journey I discover that the roads aren't as bad as I might have originally envisioned. Traffic is moving pretty well. Oh I know, you thought that I was going to go on and tell you about all the food in Stowe didn't you? Well I could go on and on and tell you all about it but you know what? Maybe this will just be the teaser you need to visit one day. Then you'll have a chance to check it out for yourself in Stowe ... "On Vermont Time..."

Sitting in My Grandfather's Parlor

Poetry by Roderick Bates

The sound he made clearing his throat -- not quite "autumn"
but so close that it *must* be a word;

the gray soft wool cap (the kind favored by newsboys in old movies)
that he wore on the rare occasions when he went outside;

the stratum of cigar smoke just above midway to the ceiling,
which would eddy and swirl when either of us stood;

the elastic armbands with mother of pearl fasteners just above the elbows
of his white shirt (did I ever see him in anything but a clean white shirt?);

the way he would curl his tongue and stick it out when he laughed;

the two black eyes he got when he fell down the front stairs
just weeks before he died;

his chess set, and the table where we played, and the queen
he would remove from his side;

the Philco radio beside his chair by the window,
and how he would watch one game on the ball field across the street,
while moving the dial between another two games.

More than forty years since his death,
more than ten since the house passed to me,
and still it is his front parlor,
and I feel like a visiting child --
as though he might even now call me
to pull the ash pail out of the coal furnace
and drag it out to the back shed.

Chapter 12

Gettin' Ready for Christmas 2009

By Timothy G. Stetson

The evening air has turned cool and crisp. Almost like a real December evening in Vermont is supposed to be. You see, even though it is the 4th of December, this year so far, it has seemed more like the 4th of April or the 4th of September. You can look up at Jay Peak or Mt. Mansfield and see snow but down here in the valley no snow and very warm. Just yesterday we were all able to run around outside with no jacket at all. It was that warm. Not real great for our state's tourism business but really fantastic if you love warm weather.

In Enosburg Falls tonight there is another great community get-together; the beginning of a full weekend of events that bring back memories of Christmases of old. Something you would expect when thinking of Christmas Time in New England. It is the evening of the official Christmas tree lighting where the big old pine tree on the corner of Main and Missisquoi Streets in the center of the village will be brought to life with the brand new white LED lights that surround it.

In preparation for the season, the village light crew has been busily at work putting up the lighted Christmas decorations on all the light poles around the village. There are wreaths, bells, Teddy Bears, candy canes and Christmas balls all twinkling in the cool night air. The merchants around town, especially those on Main Street, have decorated their stores all up with lights that create a scene that you might find on any picturesque Christmas card. They are all staying open a little later than normal so

Christmas shoppers, at least those who get started right away, can stop by after the tree lighting ceremony. Each merchant is hoping for a busy shopping season this year I am sure. In these economic times, they need all the business they can get.

Our little village includes quite a smattering of businesses. On Main Street we have a mattress store, Enosburg Inn & Suites, a furniture store (that incidentally has felt the pressures of a bad economy and will close right after Christmas), an art gallery and framing shop, a jewelry store, a clothing consignment shop, two drug and variety stores, an outdoor sports store, a tattoo parlor (something that is becoming very prevalent all around New England), multiple hair salons and barbers, three banks, a CD store-coffee shop combination, multiple restaurants and a newspaper office. Couple them with the four hardware – building supply stores we have in town and the other merchants located on Route 105 headed north like Family Dollar, a video rental store, the Dairy Center Restaurant, Motel, Bowling Alley and Banquet Halls, our numerous "quick stops" and you have a full shopping and dining experience right here in this little 'burg in northern Vermont.

The sounds of car doors opening and shutting are mixed with voices filled with childish excitement as families start arriving to experience the first event of the merry weekend. People come from all around the area and they range in age from the very youngest all bundled up in their strollers to the many older adults that have joined the group for the festivities yet to happen.

The President of the Enosburg Business Association welcomes everyone, steps over to the tree, locates the power cord and tells everyone to start the countdown. "10...9...8...7...6...5 ...4...3...2...1" and viola the tree comes to life with a magnificent white glow that brings a little tingle to your spine.

To highlight the lighting of the tree, we all break into song, singing the songs of the season that have been printed up on little handout sheets that we all got prior to the start of the festivities. Making a joyous noise the "sounds of the season" are heard echoing off the Main Street buildings. Voices come together and the familiar melodies are sung with love and excitement. Even those who always start a sing-along with "I can't carry a tune in a basket" are having fun and their voices mix in just fine with all the others around them to create a strong, powerful sound that can be heard up and down the village streets.

As the sounds of singing start to fade and the crowd breaks up some of us head to check out the many offerings of the village merchants. We look at furniture and dream about where the new piece might fit in our living room or our family room; we look at the jewelry and dream about which beautiful gem our lover might get us next and we admire the fine art and reminisce about all of the great artists that live in our region and feel extremely thankful that they choose to share their works right here in the middle of our little hometown.

It's been a full night of food, festivities, fun and shopping and now it's time to head home to fill the pellet stove, share a cup of hot chocolate or tea, do a little reading and get ready for tomorrow where we will experience more of "Gettin' Ready for Christmas" Weekend.

It's Saturday ....

It's Saturday morning. Wow! Still no snow ... it's a little cooler this morning but still very unseasonably warm. I just can't figure it out. I'm not complaining, just making an observation.

Today in our little 'burg in the Champlain Valley there are all kinds of Christmas events going on. Santa is greeting the community kids both young and old over at the Somerset Inn. The Enosburg Business Association has been inviting him to our little village for as long as I can remember. In fact, I even had the opportunity for more than 10 years to help him out.

Once the kids have shared their visions of new games, toys, candies and other things you can walk out under the car port at the Somerset and take a step back in history, climb on a horse drawn cart and go for a ride around the village. With bells a ringing and hoofs a clip-clopping, the Carpenter family and their team of draft horses take you on a journey through the streets of Enosburg. Many a story has been told on the ride and you get a chance to wave to all of your neighbors as you go by their homes. It is really quite fun to wave, not only to those folks you know, but to everyone you go by. There is such a feeling of community joy as you go riding through the village being pulled by those big, huge, wonderful horses. The smell of the fresh horse manure and the sounds of the sleigh bells are as much a part of Christmas as candy canes and mistletoe.

And, guess what? That's not all. There are all kinds of Christmas Bazaars and sales around the whole area. You can shop 'til you drop in true green mountain country fashion. And to top it all off, with all the great foods available around the area you are bound to not only be shopped out but full. If you live in the area, now is a great time to head home; eat some good old home cooking; and then get some rest before tomorrow's whole lineup of things to do as "Gettin' Ready for Christmas" continues.

It's Sunday ....

It's Sunday morning and the sun rises over the mountaintops on the third day of "Gettin' Ready for Christmas" weekend. I get up early to head to our church building to turn on the heat. We meet at the Masonic Building in town just like a lot of other Vermont churches and the only heat on during most of the week all winter is just enough to keep the pipes from freezing. As I head out into the cool, crisp morning air, quite different than it has been, I am reminded that it really is December. Cool little flakes of snow are starting to fall and I can feel their coolness on my forehead.

I head to the church, crank up the heat and then head home for some Sunday morning breakfast before heading back to church at around 9am to get set up. You see, I'm the Pastor which means that not only do I need to be sure the church is warm but I need to be ready to share a message of joy during this holiday season. With the group of people that attend our church that's not too difficult a task. You can feel the joy come alive as soon as they all get together...it's infectious in fact. We celebrate the season together and of course can't forget our fellowship time, something we do really well.

We often laugh at ourselves and tell others about how we eat in "True Baptist Fashion." Kind of our trademark, I guess. Just so you don't think that all we think of is our stomachs, a few weeks ago I actually preached a message called "More Than Food." We spent some time discussing what real fellowship is all about.

During the morning, plans are made to go Christmas tree shopping. Though it is not as easy today as it used to be to go trampsing through the woods and cut down the first nice pine tree you find we do enjoy packing ourselves in the car and heading to one of our area's many "cut your own" Christmas Tree Farms. It really is great to live in a place in the world where evergreens grow by the thousands.

The trip to the tree farm is always a fun one and one where we get as many members of our biological and our church families together to go tree huntin'. We grab the buck saws with their finely sharpened teeth equally spaced - are you getting a vision of some old time Vermont lumberjacks? – we hook the flatbed trailer on the truck – we can never have enough room if lots of folks come huntin' with us – locate the tie down straps in the truck and, of course, sneak the chainsaw into the back seat of the truck – "Just in case we need to be doing a little trimmin' after the successful hunt.

We all get together and head off on our annual journey down the highway – Route 108 to be exact. Within a few short minutes we are there. The Bakersfield Tree Farm in yup you guessed it the little town of Bakersfield, a community about 10 miles south of Enosburg.

Bakersfield is one of those towns that Kathy has always really liked. It is a storybook like town that possibly time really has forgotten. It is a bedroom community that is home to some of the nicest people around.

As we pull into the parking lot that during the summer serves as the front lawn for the family that owns the tree farm we are met by familiar scenes of Christmases of today and yesteryear – the wreaths are hanging on the shed, a mechanical Santa and a singing reindeer set up around the yard welcome young and old alike and provide a great opportunity to be a "kid" again no matter how old. There are signs all over the tree farm reminding would be Christmas Tree Lumberjacks to watch their step and not step on the little baby Christmas trees that are starting their lives in between the bigger more adult trees.

Evergreens of all shapes, sizes, and types stand at attention in perfect, carefully planned and cared for rows. You can tell that each tree is tended to all year long with love and care. The sweet smell of pine is everywhere stirred up by the fresh cutting that is happening all around the fields of the farm. You can't always see the people but you can hear the family discussions taking place as the slight breeze carries the voices across the vast flatness of the tree farm the sound baffled only by the trees themselves.

We snake our way around the rows.

"Wow!, this one looks good."

"No it's too tall."

"This is the one we want."

"Naw, that one's too short."

"Hey what about this one?"

"That's the one."

"Finally"

"Perfect"

Out comes the buck saw and down comes the tree ...timberrrrr. We got us a Christmas tree. Four more tossed on the pile to be picked up by the flatbed and we are on our way. Our "Gettin' Ready for Christmas" weekend has gotten us a little closer to a good old time Christmas ... "On Vermont Time..."

Chapter 13

My Great-Grandmother the Witch

By Lou Hill

Vermont writer Joseph Citro, author of "Green Mountain Ghosts, Ghouls and Unsolved Mysteries" and "Passing Strange," often bemoans the fact that he has never experienced any paranormal events similar to those which play such an important part in his writing, both fiction and non-fiction. Joe has never seen a ghost, nor has he ever encountered one of the strange creatures that are said to inhabit the forests of the Green Mountain State. He has never been abducted by aliens much less spotted a UFO. However, if you are ever able to attend one of his speaking engagements, you might be fortunate enough to hear the story about the time he "thought" he had seen a UFO.

In that respect Joe and I are kindred spirits. I have never experienced anything that could be considered fodder for "The X Files" or "Unsolved Mysteries." But I have just discovered something that puts me one up on Joe. I have a great grandmother who was a witch! Yes a bonafide, tried and convicted witch of the 17th century.

Those of you who may have read a story that I wrote a few years back called "Shaking the Family Tree" know that I am a dyed-in-the-wool genealogy nut. Recently I made an excursion to the Vermont Historical Society's Library located in the old Pavilion Building in Montpelier. This outstanding collection of material includes a number of volumes of various family histories. While browsing through the shelves I discovered a fairly large volume on the Foster family, one of the "limbs" of my tree. I located the pages which referred to one of my grandfathers, Andrew Foster, and found quite a bit written about him. However, it was the information on his wife, Ann Foster, which caught my eye. According to the author she had been tried, convicted of witchcraft, and sentenced to death by hanging. Her crimes: bewitching a hog belonging to John Lovejoy, causing the death of one of Andrew Allen's children, making another child sick and "hurting" Timothy Swan. Crimes to which she readily confessed.

According to the book her manner of hurting was to make images of persons with rags called "poppets" She would then stick pins in them, or "tie knots in the rags," or burn them in the fire. The persons who these images were supposed to represent would suffer whenever she pinched or burned or pricked the "poppet."

In addition to the aforementioned "crimes," she described extraordinary apparitions which she had seen. "Birds with great eyes which first were white and became black when they flew away, by which she knew they were devils." She claimed to have been at witch meetings and seen over 300 witches.

All this took place not in Salem as one might expect, but rather in Andover, Massachusetts. The year 1692, during the peak of the witchcraft frenzy.

Ann Foster was an aged woman, recently widowed and by all accounts, extremely pious. So pious, in fact, that there is little doubt that she was led to charge herself with the sin of witchcraft in all sincerity and contrition. She was evidently weak in mind and body, although seven years earlier she had acted with efficiency as the executrix of her husband Andrew's estate, and was ready at the trial to confess almost anything and to believe everything which was suggested against herself. Imagine this poor, tottering, feeble creature, dragged from her home, thrown in jail and then "examined" at length on four different days, July 15, 16, 18, and 21.

Time and time again she repeated her confession of these crimes, but on one point she was obstinate. She would accuse herself to any extent but she would not accuse her daughter even though her child later admitted that she was a witch and blamed it on her mother's influence.

"Your daughter (Mary Foster Lacey) was with you and Goody Carrier when you did ride upon the (broom) stick?"

"I did not know it."

"How long have you known your daughter to be engaged (in witchcraft)?"

"I cannot tell nor have I any knowledge of it at all."

"Do you not acknowledge that you did so?"

"No and I know no more of my daughter's being a witch than what day I shall die upon."

Mary Warren, one of those who claimed to have been afflicted by the witches, testified that Goody Carrier's "shape" told her that Goody Foster had made her daughter a witch.

Despite the denial of Ann Foster, Mary Foster Lacey alleged that it was true that they were both witches, and she cried out: "O mother, we have left Christ and the devil hath got hold of us."

However it was the testimony of Ann's grand-daughter that was most damning.

When the younger Mary Lacey was brought in to testify, Mary Warren fell into a violent fit.

Q: "How dare you come in here and bring the devil with you to afflict these poor creatures?"

Lacey laid her hand on Warren's arm and she recovered from her fit.

Q: "Can you look upon that maid, Mary Warren, and not hurt her? Look upon her in a friendly way?"

She trying to do so, struck her down with her eyes.

Q: "Do you acknowledge you are a witch?"

A: "Yes."

Q: "How long have you been a witch?"

A: "Not above a week."

Q: "Did the devil appear to you?"

A: "Yes."

Q: "In what shape?"

A: "In the shape of a horse."

When offered a chance to be saved, to which young Mary readily agreed, she was told "Then you must confess what you know freely in this matter."

She then proceeded: "I was in bed and the devil came to me, and bid me obey him. I would want for nothing and he would not bring me out."

Mary Lacey, my first cousin eight times removed, went free. Mary Foster Lacey, my seven times great-grandaunt, was condemned but spent only a short time in jail. She died June 18, 1707. It was my eight times great-grandmother, Ann Foster, who was condemned as a witch and sentenced to hang. She died in jail, probably late in 1692, before the sentence could be carried out.

Chapter 14

Odocileus Virginianus

By Lou Hill

Today, in order to purchase a hunting license, it is necessary to produce evidence of previously holding a hunting license or a certificate indicating that you have passed an NRA approved Hunter Safety Course.

Many older hunters, like myself, have held licenses for years and were "grandfathered" in. A great number of these older hunters never attended hunter safety classes. Most of them, however, had a parent or other relative who taught them the basic principles of hunter safety.

I had three teachers in my early years that I remember vividly. One was my great-uncle, Minot Austin, who taught me the "do's and don'ts" of handling a loaded weapon. Uncle Minot gave me my first gun when I was ten. It was a long barreled 12 gauge shotgun made by Springfield Arms and used by the Vermont Home Guard during World War II. Like most 12 gauge shotguns, it killed at both ends but since I was always a big kid (I wasn't overweight, I was under-tall) the kick never bothered me that much. It was a single shot; you broke it open with a lever to load and unload, and in order to cock it, it was necessary to pull the hammer back with your thumb. More than once, when my hands were numb with cold, I lost the hammer as I went to shoot at a partridge and blew holes in the trees when it went off at waist level, spinning me around like a top.

Another teacher was my great-grandmother, Sarah Austin, who was in her late seventies. Gram Austin always cautioned me about making sure of what I was shooting at whenever I left the house with my gun. Good advice in those days when it was not uncommon to hear stories about the local eateries with tales of "sound shots" during deer season. Strangely, according to the stories, they were always from Massachusetts. We never seemed to have non-resident hunters from any other place in those days. Odd.

Gram always insisted that I clean my shotgun each time I came in from the woods even if I hadn't shot it. My cleaning kit for the 12 gauge consisted of a long string, a clincher type sinker, some soft flannel cloth and a can of 3-in-1 oil. I would cut a cleaning patch out of the flannel and tie one end of the string to it. The sinker would be attached to the other end of the string, dropped onto the barrel, and the patch, with a few drops of oil squirted on it, pulled through the barrel until the bore was clean and shiny.

It took a little practice to learn to cut a patch just the right size. Too big and it couldn't be pulled through the barrel, too small and it wouldn't remove all the powder residue.

After I had cleaned the gun, Gram would check to make sure that I had done a thorough job. She would pick up the gun, break it open, and with the barrel pointed to a light, she would squint up one eye and peer through it to make sure that I hadn't missed anything. To this day, I get a guilty conscience if I don't clean a gun as soon as I use it.

Later, when I went to high school, I was fortunate to get an even better education in Hunter Safety and woods lore. At that time (late 1940's – early 1950's) George R. Tyler was principal at Enosburg Falls High. Since deer season always started on November 14 back then, it frequently fell on a school day. Mr. Tyler would excuse us from school on opening day provided we attended a gun safety course and passed a test.

Mr. Tyler was an avid hunter and an NRA member. He was our only instructor for the first few years, but, later on, brought in several other instructors including Frank Wood, a local businessman and former FMI firearms instructor, who brought in his extensive gun collection and shared his expertise with us.

In addition to teaching gun safety, Mr. Tyler taught us how to field dress a deer, tracking and general information about deer and their habits, conservation and Vermont's hunting regulations. One thing I remember well was Mr. Tyler's habit of putting the Latin name for white tail deer on the black board at the opening session each year. Odocileus Virginianus!

The course was held weekly during activity period for six weeks prior to opening day. The final class was a written test which we had to pass in order to get the excused absence. The passing grade was 100%. Mr. Tyler always said "there is no room for error with a loaded gun." Actually the test wasn't that difficult. By my senior year I had taken it so many times I could have answered the questions without seeing the test.

Shortly before the opening day of the 1952 season, a photographer/writer came to school and took pictures of the class. He wanted one of the students to dress up in "appropriate attire" and go out in the woods for pictures. I was elected, but since my hunting gun was my old 12 gauge shotgun, Mr. Tyler loaned me his rifle complete with scope and sling. This was a pretty exotic firearm in a day when a Winchester Model 94 was the gun that most of us dreamed of owning.

The photographer shot a large number of pictures in color. He said that they "might" be used for an article on hunting for the Boston Globe's Sunday rotogravure section. As far as I know, the Globe never used the pictures or ran an article. So much for my 15 minutes of fame.

Mr. Tyler did write an excellent article "Education for Hunting" which appeared in the September, 1953 edition of "The American Rifleman", a copy of which I still have. I'm sure that Mr. Tyler's course and the article that he wrote helped to promote the NRA's fledgling Hunter Safety Course and ultimately led to the requirement for passing a Hunter Safety course prior to being issued a license.

I don't hear too many stories about "sound shots" anymore so it must be working. And I'll never forget the "Ten Commandments of Firearms Safety" or that a white tail deer is also known as "Odocileus Virginianus."

Morning Is

Poetry by Lauren L. Young

LIGHT CASTS ITS FIRST SHADOW
A NEW DAY DAWNS
IN THE MORNING DEW
THE MOUNTAINS YAWN

THE AIR IS CRISP
BUTTERNUTS HIT THE GROUND
FEET POUND THE PAVEMENT
SQUIRRELS MAKE THEIR ROUNDS

SILENCE IS BROKEN
DISTANT HUES
RUMBLE OF LIFE
GEESE FLYING ON CUE

SWIRLS OF COLOR
LIGHTING UP THE SKY
MORNING IS
BEAUTY TO THE EYE

THE DARK NIGHT RECEDES
GIVE GLORY FOR THIS DAY
HOPE BRINGS A SMILE
LIGHTING THE WAY

Chapter 15

"It's Franklin County Field Days Time Again"
"On Vermont Time…"

By Timothy G. Stetson

The roar of the antique tractors just subsided as the parade of the large, steel relics of agricultural yesteryear bathed in colors known as implement colors return to the display area on the grounds of the Franklin County Field Days where they are on static display all weekend long for spectators young and old to see, mull over and learn about. There are tractors made by John Deere, Farmall, Oliver, Case and many, many other manufacturers and the implements to complement them and even a few other antique engines to boot. Many a story is shared by an old Vermont farmer who remembers using these antique pieces when they weren't antique but were brand new and the modern equipment of the day.

So what's a Field Day you say? Many people have asked that same question   Well, it can be described as many things. It is an outdoor event that is a little larger than a community carnival but smaller than the largest of fairs – in Vermont being the Champlain Valley Fair and the Vermont State Fair. I think the best way that I can describe a Field Day is as a Country Fair with all the fixin's. A fun place to take the family that doesn't cost an arm and a leg but provides for bushels of fun.

The Franklin County Field Days, for example, in addition to the Antique Tractor and Engine display has dairy barns; horse barns with some really huge percheron work horses all the way to the beautiful quarter horses and more; displays of oxen and dairy cows; 4-H exhibits, a Petting Zoo, a midway with rides and games; many commercial exhibits; a food row where every kind of fair food you can think of is available; a homemakers building,; arts and crafts; a sugar house; a main stage with live entertainment throughout the weekend; and much, much more.

Oh and we can't forget the favorite events of most field days: oxen and horse pulling; tractor, truck and antique tractor pulling, demolition and super 8 derbies; oxen, horse and pony pulling and even a snowmobile race without snow – known, of course as the grass drags. This is in addition to the pedal tractor pulls and pedal tractor grand prix for the kids; 4-wheeler ATV Pulls and side by side races. There are a whole slew of events and displays all meant to educate, entertain and otherwise keep the patrons of the field days busy.

The field days are great places for young and old to learn about the dairy industry, maple sugar making and all other kinds of agricultural business all in one place over the period of one weekend.

The vendors at the event range from the local car dealer to the tractor and farm implement dealers from around the whole county and beyond. We also can't pass by the maple sugar making equipment dealers. Never know when you want to pick up a new arch or boiling pan or a complete hobby unit – brand new and shiny.

Did I mention the fair food? I know I did in a previous paragraph but did I mention all the different kinds of fair food that are available right here at just the Franklin County Field Days? There's burgers and fries; hotdogs and sausages; salads and grinders; pies, ice cream, and "Kettle Korn"; baked potatoes, Mexican delights and Philly Cheesesteaks all to be topped off by your favorite beverage including soda, water, milkshakes or even a beer or two from the saloon. No matter what your taste buds are looking for, it is all available from this county country fair of country fairs – the Franklin County Field Days.

So if you are taking a trip to Vermont or maybe you even live here, be sure to check out one of the county field days if they happen to be occurring when you're here. You will be glad you did…"On Vermont Time…"

Barney Malone leading the Parade of Antique Tractors

Last Frost of Summer

Poetry by Roderick Bates

This morning I spend time I didn't really have,
looking for my scraper –
Summer ends this weekend,
but today I'll be late for work
if I don't find
the damn scraper soon.

Grass is stiff on my lawn, and anyone
who left basil out last night won't have to worry
about where to put all the pesto.

After a quick trip through the garage,
I dig deeper in the truck, and find one –
red plastic the size of a credit card,
Budweiser printed on the side.
It won't handle January's worst,
but it is fine for today.

The shavings curl up onto my fingers,
which are stiff with the cold
by the time I am ready to drive away.

I glide through town slowly, hunched over
to see out the bottom third of the windshield,
as my heater slowly clears away the fog
on the inside of the glass.

Next time I will start the car first,
will know where the scraper is,
will have switched to winter washer fluid
to melt what the scraper can't reach.

Next time, it will be Fall,
and I will be ready for Winter.

Chapter 16

Fourth of July in Enosburg

By Lou Hill

For many years Enosburg and Richford alternated 4th of July celebrations. While I never went to the Richford doings, I wouldn't think of missing the events here in Enosburg.

One of the highlights of the day was the parade. In addition to the usual farm related floats, local bands, veterans groups, etc. there was often an appearance by The Blackwatch Bagpipers. They were the first pipe band that I ever saw and are still my favorite.

Clad in kilts made from their distinctive black and green clan plaid, they were an imposing sight. They all seemed to be giants from my perspective, an impression probably strengthened by the jaunty angle at which they wore their tams.

But the pipes, ah the pipes, I still get chills when I hear bagpipes played. I don't remember and probably never knew, the names of the tunes that they piped. I do know that the sounds of those bagpipes raised the hairs on the back of my neck something that still occurs when I hear something that really moves me. The only other tune I have heard played on the pipes that I remember affecting me more was "Amazing Grace" piped at a police officer's funeral.

It wouldn't have been the 4th without fireworks. Although at that time, they had been illegal in Vermont for several years, there were always some to be found. I remember that "Peanut" Kennison usually managed to get a large quantity of fireworks and was willing to part with some for the "right price." So I was not deprived of the thrill of having a firecracker singe my fingers when the lighted fuse burned at an unexpectedly high rate of speed.

For me, one of the best parts of the whole celebration was the annual "water polo" match between the Enosburg and Richford fire departments. This game resembled water polo about as much as I resemble Robert Redford. Main Street was blocked off and snow fences erected on each side of the street the length of the park and the cemetery opposite. A pumper from the Richford department was stationed at one end of the cordoned off area and a pumper from the Enosburg department at the other. Two hose lines were run from each pumper. Goal lines and a center line were drawn on the street. The ball used was about the size of a regulation soccer ball and was completely white.

The rules of the game were simple. Each team tried to propel the ball into its opponent's goal area utilizing streams of water. If the ball was trapped in two opposing streams of water and wouldn't move in either direction, the referee would call for a centerline face off. The referee kept the game under control – more or less.

Each hose was manned by a three man team. Enosburg usually had the four Kennison brothers, Hazen, Rollie, Richard, and Darrel involved as well as Harry Towle and Wilbur Wright. I'm not sure if the intent of the game was to score points or drown the spectators. The ball frequently was held up against the snowfence by the force of the water, showering everyone in a twenty yard radius. The referee seemed to make sure that the crowd was thoroughly soaked before calling for a face off. I remember Wilbur Wright was notorious for turning his hose on the crowd ignoring the ball completely.

There was no curb on the cemetery side of the street and consequently the street had lots of small stones and other debris on it. Naturally when hit by the high pressure hose, this debris flew everywhere hitting players and spectators alike. Fortunately, no one was ever seriously hurt, although I do remember Wilbur Wright taking the full force of one of the hoses square in the face. I'm sure his eyesight was blurred for several days after.

Alas today the parades are smaller, the Black Watch no longer pipes, there are not fireworks popping around your feet or scorching the fingers of the unwary and no more "water polo."

The Eyes of Night

Poetry by Lauren L. Young

Tis the magic of summer
The birds are in tune
In awe, I am
Of the golden moon

Moonbeam crossing
Stars shining bright
Floating
Breathless delight

Campfires dot the shoreline
Water splashes over me
I stifle a giggle
My spirit is free

Among the stars
I see moving red lights
Wings on high
Fly through the night

A fish jumps
Frogs serenade
The air is warm
In the water I wade

A presence I feel
My heart pounds
I stop and listen
To nature's sounds

Looking up at the vast sky
I am a tiny spec
Such a grand view
I shall never forget

Wrapped in serenity
Moments to treasure
The Symphony of Silver Lake
An abyss of pleasure

Chapter 17

The Old Swimming Hole

By Lou Hill

I feel sorry for kids who never had the opportunity to swim in a place like Kidder's Hole. They missed an important part of growing up that I took for granted.

Kidder's is a classic swimming hole, one found in a Rockwell painting. Rarely do you find as pretty a spot, the clear water flowing between high rock ledges. Flatlanders used to the brackish, slow moving streams of Illinois, Ohio and other mid-western states will never know the joy of standing in a waterfall on a hot August afternoon with thousands of gallons of water pouring onto your head.

Like many of my friends, I spent most of the summer daylight hours at Kidder's. From the time school was out until Labor Day, we could be found in various stages of undress, laying on the rocks, jumping into the pools or just happily floating in the water.

Kidder's had many firsts for me. I learned to swim there. Bobby Garrett and Doug Kittel taught me in the time-honored tradition; they threw me off one of the ledges into the deep pool. They had also taught me how to eat dirt a few years earlier by throwing me off the old gravel pit near the Grange Hall. I may have been one of the originators of dwarf throwing.

I also learned to smoke at Kidder's, an experience shared with many others before and after me. I think I started out smoking Philip Morris cigarettes, probably because I could steal them from my Aunt Doris. My mother didn't smoke in those days and my step-father, Johnny Pomeroy, would have killed me if I had stolen his Camels. Old Golds and Pall Malls rated high too.

One of the big attractions of Kidder's are the ledges, towering over both sides of the hole. They provide a perfect launching point for diving and jumping. Heights vary from 10 to 40 feet above the water. You picked the height depending on how brave, or how dumb, you were. Most of us chose to jump or dive from the lower ledges.

For the very brave or foolhardy, depending on your viewpoint, the ultimate test was the high ledge. It is a little point of rock jutting out from the bank just as you come down the hill from the road. It is at least forty feet above the surface of the water. It is mossy and slippery and difficult to step out on, brush grows up out of it and there used to be an old dead tree sticking up in the air about ten feet.

Johnny Billado and one of his older brothers used to climb up into the tree to get as far above the water as possible. Johnny, who was always small for his age, would crawl up onto his brother's back and lock his arms around his neck and his legs around his waist. Johnny's brother would dive out of the tree, and as they fell, Johnny would release his hold and they would both slice cleanly into the water. I could never get up enough nerve to jump off that ledge, much less think about diving.

I did jump off all the other ledges including the narrow higher ledge on the right. This ledge is about 30 feet above the water. When you jump off from it you must jump out and away in order to clear the ledges below. I was a real menace when I jumped off that ledge. Since I have been blind as a bat since age seven, I rarely had any idea what was happening in the hole below. I would take a few running steps and launch myself off the ledge with little regard to who was below. Since I was always a tad on the heavy side, the shock waves I generated when cannon balling into the water were apt to founder any small child dog paddling in the area. The worst thing that happened was making a direct hit on a swimmer half my size and half drowning him.

Another sport was bottom walking. This entailed selecting a rock large enough to overcome your body's natural buoyancy and walking underwater as far as you could without coming up for air. In my day, Bucky Farr was unequaled. He could start at the shallow end and walk up to the flat rock at the entrance to the "channel". He would surface take a few breaths, dive down some forty feet, pick up the rock and return to his starting point. This from a man who smoked like a chimney; Imagine what he could have done if he hadn't smoked at all.

A few years ago I brought my wife Gwen, daughter Lesli and her husband Rick up to Kidder's to show them where a part of my life had been spent. Rick and I jumped off some of the lower ledges then climbed up on the higher ledges to get some sun. I kept looking down from the thirty foot or so height of the ledge and the thought crossed my mind "should I?" and a little voice said "what the heck" and off I went.

Fortunately, there was no one directly below me and some instinct unused for forty years surfaced and I remembered to jump out and away from the rocks below. Since I am still a tad overweight, I hit the water with a satisfying splash. Needless to say my wife volubly questioned my sanity and I walked around all day with my chest puffed out, macho image intact.

December 30

Poetry by Roderick Bates

I lug the last half cord
of firewood into the shed.
I have to whack some chunks
with the maul, as they are frozen
to one another or to the ground.
Snow crusts the backyard,
although the front lawn is green.

Next I lean the ladder,
remove the rain gutter
from the northern pitch.

I hang the ladder in the garage.
While I'm there, I pull the batteries
from my wife's motorcycle
and from mine.
I tote them into the house,
store them on the cellar stairs.

I have finished Winter preparations,
barely in time to avoid making
a New Year's Resolution.

My wife notes that Fall
was the time for final tasks.
She shakes her head
at a pattern of carelessness.

I say that when the Solstice came,
I stared Old Man Winter
hard in his angry, ice-blue face,
and by God,
I stared him down.

It isn't carelessness, Woman;
It is style.

Chapter 18

"Cider Pressing"
"On Vermont Time…"

By Timothy G. Stetson

It's been a long time coming but the steel cider press that has been sitting out in back of our house here in Enosburg is starting to look like a real cider press rather than a metal stick figure growing out of the ground.

The cider press' new life began about 2 years ago when my son Dave, who was having a discussion with a family friend, John, about apple orchards and cider presses, mentioned to John that I was interested in getting a cider press. John was quick to respond that he had a cider press frame that he would be willing to give me as he was thinking about purchasing a whole new unit. With that quick "spur of the moment" discussion my dream of my family and I being able to press our own cider was on its way to fruition ("No pun intended.").

We chose a Saturday, not too long after that discussion happened, to take a trip to John's to pick up the press frame. Even as excited as I was, I prepared myself for the fact that we might find a cider press made out of old auto parts or almost anything and I was pleasantly surprised to find, sitting next to the road, a cider press frame that was made out of tubular steel that looked exactly like most of the wooden cider presses that I had been checking out during my research phase and had envisioned in my many early night dreams as I thought about the fun of pressing cider.

John jumped off the tractor that he was using to do some work on one of his trout ponds that sit next to the newest orchard that he had just planted. He joined us out by the press frame and shared some stories with us about how the press was actually designed and made. You see, he was a teacher in the industrial arts program at the local Vocational Center and one of the projects he had assigned to a class of students was to design and build a cider press for him. Well they did their homework and came up with a press that they could make out of steel that resembled a cross between a large commercial cider press and the typical wooden frame presses that you can find on the Happy Valley Ranch website on the internet.

John laughed as he told the stories of how he, his family and a group of his neighbors each year would get together for a cider pressing party. He said it took quite a bit of work to press the cider. You see, when the students engineered the method of attaching the threaded rod to the press, they decided to use large nuts that matched the threaded rod. They wanted to be sure that the press and rod were sturdy so they welded on six of these huge nuts and threaded the rod through them. "Wow, Did all of those nuts make it hard to turn!" John said that he did find that the longer each party went on, the easier the rod seemed to turn. Seems that not much other than a sap bucket with holes in it was used as a pressing bucket but that worked well for what John's neighborhood wanted to accomplish. A batch of apples, a holy sap bucket, some filter cloth and a catch bucket and they were on their way to sweet success.

With the fun stories under our belt and with the help of both of my sons and another family friend we loaded the cider press frame on the back of our Ford F-250, prepared it for the trip to our house and off we went.

Once we got it home we off loaded it and hefted it out to the backyard next to the greenhouse. I had a chance to do a little cleaning of the steel but even though the frame was now right in my backyard it seemed that every time I thought about buying the rest of the materials I needed for the project something else came up that I needed to spend the money on. I couldn't always spend the money that I needed to but I sure spent a lot of time searching the internet for new and old ideas alike and amassed quite a bit of knowledge about what I needed to do to make the frame into a workable cider press.

Finally after having the frame for a couple of years I was able to start ordering all of the parts that I needed to take the "long-time" dream and that steel frame and turn it into an honest to goodness cider press. I ordered a pressing bucket and pressing disc from Happy Valley and after some glitches in shipping I ended up with not only the pressing bucket and disc but also a pressing tray. Now all I needed as far as accessories was the pressing grate better known as a juicerack, some pressing/filter bags and a couple of plastic buckets. Oh yes, and I can't forget the Easy-Do food safe poly-urethane that I need to poly all of the wood parts with and the food safe lubricating grease that I need to keep the threaded rod moving smoothly through the one nut that is left without tainting the cider.

One nut you say? Yes I almost forgot the fun my brother-in-law Albert; his son and my nephew Kraig and I had cutting off five of the six nuts to make the threaded rod turn a whole lot easier. I hauled the whole frame up to his garage, in Franklin, where he was fully equipped with the welding and cutting equipment we needed for the task at hand – making the threaded rod easier to turn. We cut four of them right completely off and left one on the rod at first, just in case. Eventually, it too, was cut off leaving us with only one nut on the whole frame.

Even with Albert's welding skills, in this case cutting skills, it took us quite a bit of time to get the nuts off without damaging the threaded rod. The rod already had a slight bend in it and we didn't want to make it worse or ruin any of the threads. The bend we can fix by cutting it off but ruined threads would mean we would have to get a new rod. Not something I want to add to the list. No problem … after some careful back-breaking work we successfully fixed the rod so it turned ever so smoothly without a ton of effort.

Now it was back to the backyard for a good "wire brushing", sanding, priming and painting. The frame got a whole new face lift and new shiny coat of Gloss Black Paint.

Remember that bend in the threaded rod I mentioned? Now it was time to fix that. You see with the addition of a pressing disc, the pressing tray, pressing rack, and wooden base we could shave off about 5 inches of that rod which would bring us pretty darn close to the portion that was perfectly straight. It seemed like another great project for Albert and I. You might think that Albert was being over asked to help on this project but you see he had an ulterior motive as well. He has a bunch of apple trees on his property and he is quite sick of having to run all the apples over with the lawn mower. He would really like to use them for some other purpose. And, he has had an interest in cider pressing for some time now. So here is his chance. If we get it done he too will realize his dream of making cider.

Out comes the reciprocating saw, off comes 5 inches of threaded rod and we are 5 inches closer to making our first batch of sweet, tasty, good old Vermont cider. One more coat of paint on the frame, poly urethane on the wooden parts and we'll be pressing.

Oh but how are we going to get the apples chopped to the appropriate size for pressing? Hmmm there seem to be tons of ideas out there about how to make an apple crusher. You can even buy them already made from companies like Happy Valley Ranch but the idea that intrigued me the most was the prospect of using a garbage disposal … yes... a brand new one with stainless steel innards to make the fine apple pulp, or pumice as the pros call it, that is needed to make the apple cider. Off to the Costco website I go to see what they have to offer. From reading the reviews online I know that many people have over-heating problems with their ½ and ¾ horse disposal units so decide to look for a 1 horse unit and lo and behold they have one. It's a Waste King 1 horse ….. I click the place order key and we're off to getting the beginnings of our apple crusher.

Though it seems like forever, within a couple of days the new shiny garbage disposal unit arrives by UPS. Now to build a stand for it…the best idea I found was to use a stainless steel kitchen sink. Figured it would serve a double purpose. I could rinse the washed apples off on one side and then crush on the other. I just happen to have a sink laying around so I grab it, make a nice plywood counter top with wooden legs and now we can crush all the apple pulp we need. A little time for some extra care being sure that I seal all of the wood to protect it from the elements outdoors as well as protecting it from the waste that is made when crushing up the apples.

Finally after all this time everything looks like it is ready. So now all we need is some apples. Off to the orchard we go. We head west on Route 105 to one of our local orchards – Vaillancourt's – and we pick some tasty Cortlands and McIntosh apples. During my research I found that mixing different flavors of apples, especially sweet and a little more tart, made for great tasting cider. We haul them home and start the process of getting them ready for pressing.

First, we have to let them set for a couple of weeks. I know, I know … we got all fired up to make cider and now we have to wait for another two weeks? I'm afraid the answer to that question is Yes. People that have been making cider for many years tell us that the two weeks gives the apples time to really produce some massive amounts of juice. Pick 'em, Let 'em sit, crush 'em and then press away.

Two weeks have gone by so now we have to wash every apple prior to slicing and grinding. This helps to assure a safe pressing. Having good clean solid apples helps us avoid bacteria. We certainly don't want anyone getting sick from our cider, that's for sure.

I know it sounds easy but it takes a considerable amount of time to wash 2 bushels of apples. But, once that is done each apple is cut into quarters to make it easier to run through the apple crusher. Whew! Then we head out back to the new shiny apple crusher that we have built. We turn it on and put the first couple of apples through. Boy, are we excited when it works. The apple spins around in the disposal but using a wooden spoon we put a little pressure on it and soon the pumice starts flowing out of the exit pipe right into our 5-gal white pail. The pumice itself looks like a fresh version of apple sauce but you can certainly see the juicy cider ready to come bursting forth.

Then, once the pail is filled up, it's time for us to pour the juicy pumice into one of the filter bags that is sitting ready and waiting in the wooden pressing basket. In it goes. We fill the filter bag to the top. Little pools of juice start to flow from under the juicerack. We twist shut the top of the bag, place the wooden pressing disc on top and start to turn the pressing screw. And viola more of the brownish colored apple juice called cider starts to flow into another set of filters in the top of the 5-gallon pail that we are using to collect our freshly made cider.

Everybody that is at our house participating in the maiden voyage of the new Stetson Family Cider Press is getting anxious now. They can't wait to taste this very first batch of cider. We pour the freshly squeezed sweetness into a pitcher and taste we all do and mmmmmm.....good the sweet taste of fresh cider hits our taste buds with a smoothness that just can't be described in words. The taste of fresh apples squeezed with loving care ... "On Vermont Time ..."

Chapter 19

Tenting Tonight

By Lou Hill

My friend, Wendall Corron, and I spent most of the summer nights of our salad days in a tent. At the time neither one of us knew that they were our salad days, in fact we didn't even know what salad days were. Webster defines salad days as "a time of youth and experience." Right on target in both cases. We were young, both teenagers although Wendall was two years my senior, and boy, were we inexperienced.

Wendall bought the tent. He had gone to work stocking shelves at Ovitt's store in West Enosburg when he first started high school so he had some ready cash. As was usual in our friendship, I was the freeloader. I did supply our bedding courtesy of my grandmother, who gave us an old feather mattress, a quilt, and some old feather pillows. We didn't bother with the luxury of sheets or pillow cases.

We pitched the tent in a patch of trees we called Preston's Woods. I'm not sure of the actual ownership of the land. It may have been partly or even completely owned by Arlin Ovitt. We never bothered to ask anyone for permission to camp there and no one ever complained about our presence.

The woods covered about an acre. They were in the bend of Tyler Branch in West Enosburg, just across from my grandmother Ada Hill's house and behind the store. The Corrons lived across the road from the Prestons so to get to our campsite we just walked up into the woods behind the Preston house.

It was just a narrow strip of trees, all pines that grew along the banks of Tyler Branch. The trees were all quite big, probably 50 or 75 years old and quite widely spaced. I doubt that they had been purposely planted as they grew in a random pattern and ran down the steep bank right into the river's edge.

There was a fairly level spot at the top of the bank and that was where we chose to pitch the tent. We set it up under the branches of a huge old pine. The ground was covered with a thick carpet of dead pine needles. The ground was pretty soft and I remember getting the tent pegs to stay in place was always a problem.

The first few weeks of camping was a learning experience for us. The most important lesson we learned was to never touch the tent walls or roof during a rainstorm. We discovered the location of several roots which entailed repositioning the tent. We also found out that the tent pegs had to be driven into the ground at an angle or they would pull out of the ground. This only occurred in the middle of a rainy night.

We soon slipped into an easy routine. We slept in the tent every night except Saturday night. Wendall had to get up early Sunday morning for Mass so his folks insisted that he sleep at home. I never stayed in the tent by myself.

We slept through some God-awful storms in that tent. Both of us were heavy sleepers and would often be surprised to awaken in the morning to discover that there had been a hard rainstorm during the night. Often, after a two or three day rainy spell, we would have to take our bedding out of the tent and lay in on the rocks to dry out.

I remember one particularly severe storm that actually woke us up. It was thundering loudly and the sky was lit up with lightning. The wind was blowing very hard and the rain was coming down in sheets. That was one of the few times that rain came in through the mesh tent flaps. By morning we were pretty wet. As soon as it let up, we hurried home to let our folks know we were alright.

We knew that they worried about us, out in the woods during storms. Of course any thoughts of danger never crossed our minds. Not because we were particularly brave either. In retrospect I guess that we were pretty lucky that a branch from one of those big old pines never came crashing down on our tent during one of those storms. Our guardian angel must have worked overtime taking care of us. He never let us down.

Although she never tried to discourage me from camping out, my grandmother was always nervous when she wouldn't see me for extended periods of time. We would usually go to our respective homes for breakfast, in mid-morning. We never got up too early, but then we often stayed up half the night. I would go home and stoke up on my usual breakfast of too many slices of toast with peanut butter and honey slathered on them, washed down with milk. Then I would be off again. If we ate supper in the woods, she wouldn't see me 'til the next morning.

She used to tell me that she watched out the living room window, hoping to see us jumping around the rocks by our favorite fishing hole. Wendall worked at the store several days a week, so his parents saw a little more of him. He would have to go home to clean up before going to work.

Our meals in the woods were a nutritionist nightmare. Our favorite was canned pork and beans usually eaten cold, sardines and as a special treat for dessert, donuts. No wonder I had a coronary by age 45.

We always had a campfire. Not that we used it much for cooking, just if you were camping you had to have a campfire.

I remember that Wendall's father was constantly reminding us to be careful with the fire and we really were. We had built a small fireplace using old bricks. After first sweeping a large area clear of dry pine needles, we built the fireplace on top of the damp, black earth under the needles. We always kept our fires very small. We didn't want to burn ourselves up and, besides, Mr Corron had said something about permanent damage to our hides if we let a fire get away from us.

One evening we were stunned to find a small plume of smoke wafting up from between the bricks we had carefully placed on the bottom of the fireplace. We hurriedly pulled them up to find a fire smoldering in the composted pine needles, much like the fires which burn for years in past bogs. Shaken, we made sure to thoroughly douse our fire each morning after that.

We usually set up the tent in the pines as soon as school let out for the year and left it there until just before Labor Day.

One year, the last of our camping, we decided to try out other spots. We pitched it up in the woods in back of Wendall's house for two or three days. I don't remember too much about that trip except that an owl woke us up one night. I swear it was perched on one of the tent posts.

We also spent a few days of that summer on the banks of what is now known as Beaver Meadow Brook in East Enosburg. The first day we fished downstream from the tent, catching scads of native brook trout which we fried up for supper that evening. They tasted much better than sardines. The next day we decided to fish upstream and discovered the remains of a porcupine in the stream about a hundred yards above the tent. We decided to stop drinking the water out of the brook after that.

What did we do in the tent on those long nights so long ago? On hot nights, we would slide down the hill and go skinny dipping in the branch at midnight. A few times Wendall's sister Helen and James Hayes, her boyfriend (now her husband of more than 40 years) would come up to spend a few hours with us. One night my cousin, John Austin, came up to camp. He told his constipated hoot owl with laryngitis story which kept me giggling for half the night, much to Wendall's disgust. We often read by the light of the flickering fire, Mickey Spillane, had just become popular then. And we talked, talked about everything under the sun as only good friends can. Since Wendall is the quiet one and I have always had a severe case of galloping mouth, I'm sure I did most of the talking. We spent a lot of time just staring into the fire too.

It's kind of ironic that Wendall and I both served in the Air Force. We would have been naturals as infantryman, living in pup tents. But that's how life goes.

Chapter 20

Gone Fishing

By Lou Hill

Like most boys who grew up in rural Vermont, I always enjoyed fishing. I am not as fanatical about it now as I used to be, but I still like to get out on a stream or a lake once in a while.

My great-uncle, Minot Austin, started me fishing when I was about six. It is the Austin genes that generate the love of hunting and fishing in my family. He cut a five foot long branch off a tree, trimmed it, wound some old fish line on the end, crimped on a split-shot sinker, then tied on a small hook. He cut the barb off the hook so that I wouldn't do too much damage to myself or anyone I accidentally hooked. I was a noted klutz even then.

We dug up some worms out in the garden and put them in an old pipe tobacco can. Those pipe tobacco cans were my bait-boxes for years; they fit into a back pocket perfectly and had a convenient cover to keep the worms from spilling out. I didn't get a fancy one that looped on a belt until I was in high school.

We headed down to the pool in the bend of Tyler Branch in front of my grandmother's house. Uncle Minot baited up with half a worm, swung the hook and line out into the water and almost instantaneously pulled out a wiggling fish. The pool was filled with trash fish: minnows, shiners, chubs; they had many names. Soon I was catching fish as fast as I could throw in the line. The fish weren't the only thing hooked.

I quickly graduated to a real fishing rod. Granted it was a hand-me-down. Uncle Minot gave me one of his old steel telescoping rods for my very own. Soon I was spending most of my time down at the branch, perfecting my fishing technique.

It was about this time that I met my lifelong friend, Wendall Carron. Wendall was as crazy about fishing as I was, but in his case fishing was serious business as it often provided a meal for his family.

For the next ten years, Tyler Branch and trout fishing were the center of our lives. Both of us hunted, but we lived for fishing. In the summer, not a day went by that we didn't spend a few hours fishing. In the winter we spent most of our time talking about fishing.

We were pretty good fishermen too, we could always catch trout even on the hot days of summer when the water was low and they were particularly difficult to get to bite. We had our favorite tricks and methods, one of which would usually work.

One evening about a year after the end of WWII, we spotted someone fishing in our favorite hole. We considered this spot our own personal property. We called it the "big hole," not a very original name. Naturally we investigated to find out who had had the nerve to invade our territory.

The fisherman was Arnold "Curly" Kittell, an Enosburg man who had moved to Connecticut during the war. Curly was a well known fisherman and we had heard many stories about his abilities when it came to trout fishing.

We were anxious to find out his methods, so we struck up a conversation. Curly was not the least bit secretive and told us everything we wanted to know. He was using tackle exactly like ours, steel rod, bait casting reel with black silk line, etc. However, he had attached about a three foot gut leader (the forerunner to mono-filament) to the silk line with a small barrel swivel. He opened his cloth fishing bag and showed us the bait he was using.

Lying on top of a folded seine were about a dozen small minnows. Curley called them "sucker minnows"; they had a mouth like a sucker, were about three inches long, slim with a black stripe down the side. They spawned in early August and Curly had netted them as they tried to jump up the falls.

He would thread the minnow on the hook in such a way that the minnow would spin when trolled on the surface. The barrel swivel kept the line from twisting.

We watched as he stood on the ledge and cast the minnow way downstream and then pulled the line, hand over hand, through the guides bringing the minnow up stream. The minnow could be seen, spinning on the surface, leaving a small wake.

Suddenly, as we watched, the minnow vanished. Curly waited while the trout swallowed the minnow, then set the hook. He battled the huge fish for at least ten minutes, then, like a teenager, he jumped down the slippery ledges, stuck his finger in the gills and lifted a twenty inch brown trout out of the water.

Wendall and I looked at each other dumbfounded. Until that moment neither of us had seen a trout that big caught much less ever having caught one. We were believers.

From then on we used "the method" extensively. We still used worms and night crawlers, but in warm weather and low water conditions, minnows worked best for us.

Wendall was the first to catch a trout longer than twenty inches, a bench mark we had established for some unknown reason. In fact I never managed to break that barrier. I came close though.

One night in early August I was fishing alone, Wendall was in the service and I was going to be in my last year of high school that fall. I was using "the method." As I trolled a minnow up the brook below the big hole, a huge fish rose up and swallowed the bait. I let the fish take the line, then set the hook. The rod bowed under the weight of the largest fish I had ever had on a line.

Suddenly everything went slack. The fish was gone. I reeled in and looked at my line. All that was left was the barrel swivel on the end of the silk line. The knot attaching the leader to the swivel had come untied. Because of my carelessness, I had lost my trophy.

The next year I went into the service. Wendall had been sent to Alaska and spent most of his spare time fishing. I ended up being sent to Korea and spent most of my time griping.

I did luck out when I came home from Korea in the spring of 1956. It was, I believe, the first year that trout season opened on the fourth Saturday in April instead of the first day of May and I got home just in time for the opening day. Of course I hit the branch right off. It was a bitter cold day as I remember. No one, myself included, seemed to be having much luck.

For some reason, just before giving up around noon, I tried a hole that had never been too productive for me. This time I hit the jackpot. In five minutes I had a pair of matched rainbows, sixteen inches long, weighing about three pounds apiece, in my creel. That's what fishing is all about.

Chapter 21

Growing Up In Vermont

By Lauren L. Young

I saw a t-shirt last week on a gal in the grocery store. It said, "If you're good and say your prayers, when you die you will go to Vermont." The owner of the t-shirt wouldn't give it to me, but she told me where I might be able to get one.

Raising children in Vermont allows you many opportunities when you're pursuing adventure with your child. It's all free. Libraries and museums are excellent choices, but if you can't get there for whatever reasons, you can always go for a walk; a simple walk downtown with your youngster can turn into an educational experience. Signs are various shapes, octagons, squares, circles, triangles and rectangles. It's fun to teach them. Believe me they won't forget; in fact, they will proudly share their new knowledge with grandpa, Aunt Sue or big brother John when they are riding down the road with them.

Look up, the clouds in the sky tell a story. Beyond cumulus (cum-u-lus is fun to say), stratus, cirrus, and counting syllables, is a panoramic view of pictures in clouds. Last summer I was on Lake Carmi in a boat. I looked up at the cum-u-lus clouds, and two dogs loomed overhead. A Scottish terrier was being chased by a Labrador who was leaping out from behind the tree tops.

A child is always thirsty for knowledge, and you as parent are privileged to be their first teacher. Their thirst is insatiable and it all begins with you. You are given the opportunity to provide them with quality learning experiences. Providing a home for your child requires you to be away from them, but remember it is quality not quantity that makes the difference. There really is a time to play and a time to work.

A picnic adventure provides an opportunity to ignite their creative juices. Pick up a rock or stone and turn it over and over in your hands and magic, you are now holding a dog, lion, shoe, boat, turtle, horse, an endless collection. As your children grow into the fraction of population we call teenagers and they balk at doing their chores at home, you can always threaten to get out the rock collection the next time their friends are over. Persuasion tactics or blackmail, it works.

"Mom, not the rocks again." I'll pick up my room now, I promise."

But sometimes you just can't resist a chance to dig them out from the closet and share the gems of creation with anyone you can snag, as they are helplessly walking by.

Bedtime stories, treasured moments – Gather everyone. Choose a cozy corner, a bed or your favorite place. Grab some pillows and start your story. Let each one add to it if they want to. You may offer direction, but their own spices will add flavor to the tale they are brewing. What a story. You'll see. A delectable hearty tale will unfold. As food nourishes our body, enhancing creativity feeds the mind.

Bringing a child up today isn't easy, but the activities I have mentioned will ease the tension of child rearing. Guidelines – a child needs guidelines with a dab of discipline. Remember, you are the parent, not the child. Sometimes being an authority figure costs you popularity votes, but it's important for your sanity and peace of mind to discipline your child, when needed, using firm positive action. A favorite line my teenagers would throw at me was this.

"Who cares?" or "I don't care."

Guaranteed to send my blood pressure up.

I'd look them in the eye (eye contact is very important) and say to them, enunciating in a clear and firm tone, "You do care, because someday you could be all alone, and if you don't care, who will."

Unfortunately, bringing up children sometimes causes a lot of pain and anger. Offer a learning and loving environment for them, a place for them to feel safe and warm. Give them responsibilities. Teach them to respect themselves and others. Make sure they understand that it's okay to make a mistake. We learn so much from our mistakes. Everyone is fallible. They are children for such a short time. When they grow up, they'll be grown up forever, but fear not, my oldest left for college in 1986. How I cried. She moved back home in 1990. How I cried. (temporarily)

In Vermont we are blessed with mountains, lakes, rivers, streams, fields of flowers, but most of all with children. Give them a hug and send them on their way. Be it off to kindergarten, high school, or college or points unknown, you tried; You did your best, the rest is up to them.

We Only Have This Moment

Poetry by Lauren Young

We only have this moment
To laugh or cry
Call a special friend
Or bake a pie.

We only have this moment
To do what must be done
Work and play
Always take time for fun

We only have this moment
To smile or frown
The choice is ours
To be up or down

We only have this moment
To please you and me
Go ahead
Plan that special party

We only have this moment
To curl up in our favorite spot
Read a book
Or go for a walk

We only have this moment
To be all you can be
Mow the grass
Of course, take time for tea!

Chapter 22

Sidehill Vermonters

By Lou Hill

Whenever we traveled during the early years of our marriage, my wife and I, like most parents of young children, would point out various sights to our daughter, Lesli, to keep her amused. On our trips from Manchester, NH to Alburg to visit my parents, her attention would most often be directed to "moo-cows." As she grew older and more difficult to distract from the boredom of a long ride, I had to become more inventive.

I finally came up with a diversion that worked for several years. I told her to watch for "sidehill" cows. Now as every "real" Vermonter knows, sidehill cows evolved on the hill farms of Vermont where many of the pastures are almost vertical. These cows are never found in the flatlands of the Champlain or Connecticut River valleys. They are rare even in the deep valley and high ridge sections of the state. Spotting one is extremely difficult.

For the un-informed, a sidehill cow can be of any breed. She has adapted to her environment by growing the legs on one side of her body longer than those on the other side. This allows the cow to graze on the sides of the steep hill farm pastures, keeping her body level without the danger of tipping over. They are true survivors. Overcoming the hardships presented by nature.

Over the years, I have come to the realization that many of the people I knew from my past and some I know at present are what I call "sidehill Vermonters." Like sidehill cows, they have adapted to their environment, overcoming difficulty, enduring hardships and personal tragedy, and doing whatever is necessary to survive.

Perhaps the best example of a sidehill Vermonter was my grandmother, Ada Hill. The eldest of four children, she was a tomboy. I have a picture of her taken shortly after the turn of the century when she was in her early teens. She is standing astride a battered girl's bicycle, hair askew, middy blouse half in and half out of the waistband of her skirt, stockings bagging at the ankles and knees. She is staring into the camera, unsmiling, a determined look on her face. That is what I remember best about her – determination.

After graduating from grammar school, she attended "Normal" school for two years in preparation for a career as a teacher. She taught for several years then married my grandfather, Louis James Hill, for whom I am named. They moved to Lewiston, Maine where they lived for over a year and where my father was born.

It must have been a lonely time for her. Tucked away in a family Bible, I found a card she had written to her grandmother in which she mentions that her husband had been away for several weeks but that she was happy to be in her warm room in the cold weather.

Sometime around 1914 or 1915 they moved to a house in Colchester. What little information I have about my grandfather is sketchy. He was a salesman for a tobacco company and apparently was one of those individuals who had some kind of a "deal" in the works most of the time. Hints of some kind of a mining scheme involving the Colchester property have filtered down through the years.

What the scheme was I will never know, because on January 8, 1916 my grandfather died, the victim of a ruptured peritonitis. After her husband's death, my grandmother moved to her parents' home in West Enosburg with her 17 month old son, my father, William Hill. Whatever his scheme had been, my grandfather had left her penniless. He had also elicited a deathbed promise from her to never remarry.

To support herself and her son, my grandmother resumed teaching in the Enosburg Town Schools. Most of her 42 years of teaching were at the West Enosburg School, where for many years, she taught all eight grades.

My grandmother was a tiny woman, barely 5 feet tall and weighing less than a hundred pounds. However, she had no difficulty in controlling a roomful of rambunctious children, usually with just a look. Often some of the hulking "big boys" were twice her size. In those days you attended school until you graduated from the 8th grade or reached the age of 16. Yet she rarely had to resort to notifying parents of a discipline problem.

When her father died, my grandmother became the support of her mother as well as of my father. After my father left home, she built all the fires, split wood, hauled ashes and cleared sooty stovepipes and did all the other chores such as gardening, etc.

When my parents divorced, I lived with my grandmother and great-grandmother for a few years just prior to WWII. Each night I would eagerly await her return from school. I would stand in the living room, nose pressed against the window, waiting for her to turn the corner in the road. My grandmother always walked to and from school. She did not drive and rarely got a ride even in the foulest weather.

I can remember her coming around the corner on bitter cold days, a heavy basket of books and papers for corrections in one hand, a bag of groceries clasped in the other arm. She would stagger into the house, shivering and barely able to move, lips blue with cold. She would never wear slacks to protect her birdlike legs as it wasn't appropriate for a woman to wear pants in her view.

She had tremendous impact on her students and she turned out many successful individuals. For many years, one of her students would be either the Valedictorian or the Salutatorian of the graduating class at Enosburg High School. When she finally retired in 1956, she received hundreds of cards and letters from former students. The underlying theme of all of them was the positive effect she had been in their lives.

Sidehill Vermonters come by the family too. When I was growing up my closest friend was Wendell Corron. Wendell was the youngest of six children. His father, Fred, was a blacksmith. He eked out a living when it cost $2.00 to shoe a horse. I doubt you can buy the nails for that price now.

The Corrons had a cow, a huge garden and usually raised a pig or two. Mrs Corron made the greatest homemade sausage I have ever eaten, my mouth waters at the thought of it. Wendell did his share, putting meat on the table. He was always bringing home fish or game. I hunted and fished for the fun of it, for Wendell it was serious. As soon as he was old enough, he got a job at the local store stocking shelves.

All four of Wendell's sisters worked their way through college. Two became teachers (my grandmother's influence) and one a nurse. Everyone in the family did what they had to do to overcome obstacles and to get on with life.

There are still many sidehill Vermonters around. I see them every day, my barber, a former teacher, the fellow who plows my driveway. They and others like them are adapting to the steep hills of life and are moving on without tipping over.

Chapter 23

Friday Night at the Movies

By Lou Hill

Enosburg has many unique things and surely one of the oldest had to be the Playhouse Theatre. Where else could you walk into a movie theatre and find yourself facing the entire audience? For a pair of teenagers on their first date, it could be an intimidating experience. All of their friends sitting there watching. So much for secret love affairs.

I went to the movies at the playhouse from the time I was six years old until after I graduated from high school. During that time nothing changed. Leslie Thomas was the projectionist, Mrs. Vincent was the "enforcer" who could quiet a bunch of rowdy teenagers with a look, and the theatre was always cold.

The format for the week was always the same too. Sunday and Monday nights were for the new releases with the big name stars; Tuesday, Wednesday and Thursday nights were "B" romances, dramas and thrillers and Friday and Saturdays were reserved for westerns.

I started going to the Friday night "oaters" when I was six years old. At that time the price of a child's ticket was about fourteen cents. At first my mother would accompany me and if the truth be known, I think she enjoyed the movies just as much as I did. I don't think she ever missed a Roy Rogers movie.

Weekends were special because they always showed the next chapter of a cliff hanger. Those old series kept people coming back week after week to see how the hero would escape from whatever life-threatening situation he had been left in at the end of the last weeks installment.

Friday night audiences were usually made up of kids from the village with a scattering of adults. Saturday night was farmer's night. A lot of the farm families would come to the "city" on Saturday evening to do their shopping. It was the only night of the week that the stores stayed open in those days. Many of them opted to take in a movie after grocery shopping. I remember that on the rare Saturday night that I went to the movies there was a distinct aroma of barn in the playhouse.

Those cowboy movies were a big part of our early education. The good guys always wore white hats; the bad guys always wore black hats. No one's hat came off in a furious fist fight. Gene Autry holds the record for most shots fired from a six-shooter without reloading (28). Western heroes are unbelievable marksmen – you try shooting a moving target when you are on a galloping horse. Good always triumphs over evil and the bad guy got punished. The hero never dies and he only kisses his horse which is not such a bad idea today.

When I saw Star Wars for the first time, I realized that the same formula was used to make it that was used for the old westerns. Bad guy (Darth Vader) in black, Obi Wan Kanobi's hood never moved when he fought Darth Vader with light sabers, Luke and Han were fantastic shots with their laser cannon even when gyrating all over space, the good guys won and the Death Star was blown up. Han Solo, like the western heroes who only kissed their horses, just exchanged meaningful looks with Princess Leia.

As I matured, so did my taste in movies. Unfortunately sometimes my actions and those of my friends didn't mature. I remember an impressive documentary film released in the early 50's called "The Fighting Lady". A group of us went to see it and proceeded to disrupt the whole theatre with additional dialogue and sound effects in the battle scenes. Even Mrs. Vincent gave up trying to quiet us down.

I also especially remember a movie called "Strangers On A Train", one of Alfred Hitchcock's great thrillers that I saw during my teens. Two things stick in my mind about that film: Robert Walker is asked by his domineering mother if he has taken his vitamins that day and he answers, "Yes mother, a whole pint of them." The other thing I remember is a very intense scene with Robert Walker prowling around looking for his intended murder victim. There was no dialogue and no loud background music. The theatre was deathly quiet; everyone was waiting for something to happen. Suddenly Richard Bordo, who was sitting next me yelled "BANG" as loudly as he could. Of course everyone in the theatre jumped out of their skins, myself included, then dissolved into nervous laughter. Mrs. Vincent never did discover the culprit even thought she patrolled the aisles for the rest of the film.

Another movie that I remember vividly was a film starring Spencer Tracy called "Mayflower Adventure" which, of course, was about the pilgrims. Tracy in his role as Captain Miles Standish was trying to teach the pilgrims how to use weapons. As he ran through a drill to load and fire a blunderbuss, he delivered the line "Pour gunpowder into the touch hole". Total bedlam in the theatre!

My favorite movies were and still are the musicals of the late 40's and 50's. I remember that I had a tremendous crush on Marge Champion of the dancing team of Marge and Gower Champion which lasted until I saw Natalie Wood in "The Searchers" and I fell in love. It was a one-sided affair that continued until her unfortunate death. Many of those old MGM musicals are considered classics today: "Easter Parade", "Meet Me in St. Louis", "The Bandwagon", "Showboat", "Seven Brides For Seven Brothers", "Singing In The Rain", etc. They didn't have a "message" for the most part, all they did was entertain.

In the last twenty years, I have only seen two movies that approach the quality and entertainment value of the old musicals. They are Flashdance and Dirty Dancing, both highly successful movies from a financial view. There ought to be a message to Hollywood hidden there.

The advent of inexpensive television sets sounded the death knell for the playhouse and many other small town movie theatres like it. In order to compete with television, movie makers have resorted to sex, more violence and my opinion, less entertainment.

On a recent Friday night, as I waited for my wife to pick up a few items at the IGA, which now occupies the building, my thoughts drifted back fifty years. Were Charles Starett and Smiley Burnett going to beat the bad guys to the pass and stop them from stampeding the herd? What new perils would face the hero of the current serial? Most important, would a Tom & Jerry cartoon be showing?

Chapter 24

Shaking The Family Tree

By Lou Hill

Webster defines genealogy as 1: "an account of the descent of a person, family or group from an ancestor or from older forms; or 2: "the study of family pedigrees." There is no mention made of the fact that tracing ones roots, or as Mr. Webster said "studying family pedigrees" quickly becomes an addiction. Maybe that's what he meant by descent of a person.

Based on the symptoms that I am exhibiting, I seem to have been bitten by the genealogy bug and have been infected with a severe case of ancestor fever. I am afraid that, unfortunately, I am nowhere near reaching the breaking point of that fever.

I avidly scan an already overfull schedule to see when I can find enough time to spend a few moments trying to locate the grave of a several times great-grandfather in a cemetery in South Hero. Can I leave for my job at the Burlington Airport a few hours early so that I can spend an hour or two at the Alburg Town Clerk's Office checking the records for a newly discovered ancestor? When I have the rare evening off on a Wednesday or Thursday night, I seriously consider a trip to the Family History Center at the Church of Latter Day Saints in Berlin to spend a few hours searching through their computer records hoping to find another name that will provide a foothold which will allow me to climb to the next branch of my tree.

Fortunately for the preservation of my marriage, my wife, Gwen, has become infected by the same bug. She is perfectly content to spend hours straining her eyes to read the microfilmed records at the Family History Center. On our first trip there, she found a significant amount of new information on her ancestors which gave her several new lines and areas to research. It also increased her feelings of frustration when she found that one of her ancestors, Peleg Sprague, had had numerous wives and a son also named Peleg thus adding to the confusion.

Like me, Gwen had suffered the effects of the "Burned Records" syndrome. When trying to find a copy of her great-grandfather Nash's application for admission to the UVM Medical School, she was told that all the records had burned up in a fire. I have been stymied by the incineration of the records of the Towns of Milton and Georgia. I have been told by veteran genealogy buffs that this is a common occurrence and in many instances is a legitimate excuse given by those responsible for the records. However in some cases it is used to disguise the lack of desire or the knowledge to find certain records.

I must be quick to add that almost everyone I have encountered when researching records has been extremely helpful and courteous. Town Clerks in particular have been very helpful, often interrupting what they were doing to get a volume from the records for me. Procedures vary from town to town. Some town clerks will give you a master index of vital statistics and then get each individual volume of records that you require. Others will point you at the records and say "have at it." A few make a minimal charge for research, others don't charge at all. Regardless, I always get more than my money's worth.

I am a tyro in the genealogy game. I started serious research only about a year ago. Just when I get cocky and think I have done well because I can trace back to my twenty five times great grand-father in the late 11th century, I get put in my place. A few weeks ago I was at the LDS Family History Center, chatting with one of the volunteers there. She mentioned that she had been able to do some work on her family tree that day, indicating a huge loose leaf binder about eight inches thick, on the desk behind her. I commented that she ought to put it in a computer. "Oh but it is" she said. "These are printouts of all the various family groups in my genealogy." "Just how far back can you trace your history?" I asked. Her answer: "To Adam."

Recently a friend asked, "Why bother tracing so far back?" A fair question, one that has many answers and one which made me do quite a bit of self examination. Why do I do it?

Probably one of the main reasons is the challenge. While it is far easier to trace one's roots in this age of readily accessible information, computers, the "Information Highway" and all that jazz, as compared to as recently as ten years ago when everything was pretty much done by on-site research or through the mail, it is still a "detective job" to piece together information, to be able to go to the right source to follow up on a clue garnered from a census record or information chiseled on a gravestone in an old cemetery. Perhaps I am a frustrated Sherlock Holmes. I certainly get a big kick out of rooting an elusive ancestor out of the mists of time by using my deductive powers.

I suppose that, like most people, I would love to find a famous ancestor in my family tree. So far, no such luck. I have found a four times great-grandfather who was a Minuteman in the Revolutionary War. My twenty five times great-grandfather, Guido de Janes, was given an estate in Essex, England by King Henry II. His grandson, Geoffry de Janes traveled to the Holy Land on three separate crusades. I have several relatives who served in various local and state offices here in Vermont. There are no well known names but I am still looking.

I sometimes find information that amuses me and often find things that sadden me as well. There have been several hastily arranged marriages, this based on the wedding date and the birth date of the first child. I have one relative who was described in "The History of South Hero" as "an eccentric genius, but more, he was a rough, untamed backwoodsman." Another distant cousin, born on the 4th of July, 1776, was named Liberty. My great-great grandfather Austin was the only one of five children to live beyond the age of three. Only one of my great-grandmother Austin's five siblings lived to maturity.

The indomitable spirit of some of my early ancestors amazes me. One of my French-Canadian ancestors, Antoine Emery, had eleven children by his first wife. All of them died at birth or shortly thereafter. When his wife died, he remarried, choosing a woman half his age. She produced nine children, all of whom lived. One of them was my six times great-grandmother, Catherine Emery.

Perhaps most amazing is the story of my six times great – grandparents, Benjamin and Hannah Janes. On May 13, 1704, Hannah and her three children were attacked by Indians at their home in Northfield, Mass. The three children were killed. Hannah was scalped and left for dead. Fortunately she recovered from her wounds and bore Benjamin six more children, including my director ancestor, Seth Janes.

As I consider the question of why I search through old records and books trying to put another twig on the tree, I find myself coming to this conclusion. History tells me who I am and it also tells me why I am what I am as well.

About the Authors

Timothy G. Stetson is a Vermont native who was born in Richford and after a short (10 year) stint in northern New York now lives in Enosburg Falls with his wife Kathy and his family. He is the Regional Disaster Program Officer for the American Red Cross in Vermont and the New Hampshire Upper Valley Region. Tim is also an ordained minister and is the Pastor of New Life Christian Church of West Berkshire, Vermont; a church that along with his wife and a team of leaders he helped plant in 2007. In addition to his work in disaster response and the ministry, Tim is a small business owner; a Gospel Music Recording Artist; performs in a Gospel Music Duo – The Stetsons; and has written two original Christian musicals for the theatre stage. Both he and his wife Kathy have been actively involved in Community Theater and many other event production projects for many years. He stays very active in many other community organizations and projects. In his 30 plus year career with the Red Cross he has traveled around the country working on some of the nation's largest disaster operations. As much as he has loved traveling to all of these places, he still loves to come home to Vermont which is why he started compiling all of the stories about the state that are found in this book.

Louis J. Hill (1935 – 2005) was born and raised in Enosburg Falls, Lou remained a Vermonter at heart while living in New Hampshire, New Jersey, New York, Texas, Missouri and Florida, and Vermont was where he returned to spend the final years of his life. While his career path included electronic engineering, sales and a stint with the INS and Border Patrol, Lou's hobbies ranged from genealogy to gemology to gardening. He was above all a life-long learner and someone who loved a good story. Inspired by a Creative Writing class taught by Vermont author Joe Citro, Lou set out to tell stories about growing up in Enosburg. His essays provide a glimpse into Vermont life with the humor and heart that were Lou's trademarks.

Roderick (Rick) Bates is a Vermont native whose family home in Chester has nurtured his forebears and his children over four generations. He has supervised the Brattleboro Probation and Parole office since 1982. He began writing poetry in high school, and became serious about it several years ago when, at his wife's urging, he joined a writing group in Walpole, NH. He also writes essays, and his essay "Straightening Nails," which first appeared in Vermont Life Magazine, won an award from the International Regional Magazines Association. He has a degree in Religion from Dartmouth College. He has published poems in Vermont Folkus, Naugatuck River Review, The Dark Horse, and on the web at Poets Against the War, Rat's Ass Review, and Astronomers Without Borders (where he won another award).

Lauren L. Young says, "Poetry flows through my veins. It feels like the calm before a storm, riding the crest of an ocean wave, and soaring through the air propelled by my own energy. Writing for me is an emotional high that whets my appetite causing insatiable hunger, which is temporarily sated with each new piece!" Through her photography she brings to the surface the five senses of touch, taste, hearing, smell and sight. Every photo tells a story; be it complex or simple, it is life. Lauren wrote her first poem when she was nine and her first story when she was in Junior High. She wrote the poem for her niece Nancy and her first story as a school assignment. She remembers fondly when the teacher asked her to approach her desk she was hoping for an "A" on the story. What she got was, "Where did you copy this from?" Because of this experience Lauren learned the importance of listening to children and teenagers. She finds her most fun writing to be when she uses romance and humor. Because if you don't have humor or romance, what do you have? She says she isn't talking about the romance between special people. She is talking about the romance of life with all its ups and downs. Sometimes you have to pull yourself up by the bootstraps and carry on. Life hands us lessons every day. What we do with them is our choice.

Photo and Drawing Credits

Timothy G. Stetson..........Pgs. 6, 10, 30, 34, 48, 62, 65, 66, 92
Harold Green...Pg. 14
Gardner Stetson (provided by Joanne Stetson) Pgs. 14, 18, 30
Kraig McFadden...Pgs. 31, 107
Lauren Young...Pg. 70
Michaela Kobyakov..Pg. 74

Even though this drawing is found on Page 31, I wanted everyone to have a chance to see a little larger version of it. My nephew Kraig McFadden drew it specifically for this book.

www.ingramcontent.com/pod-product-compliance
Lightning Source LLC
Chambersburg PA
CBHW061749020426
42331CB00006B/1411